# Black Civil Rights in America

This is an authoritative introduction to the history of black civil rights in the USA. It provides a clear and useful guide to the political, social and cultural history of African Americans and their pursuit of equal rights and recognition from 1865 through to the present day. From the Civil War of the 1860s to the race riots of the 1990s, *Black Civil Rights in America* details the history of the modern civil rights movement.

This book introduces the reader to:

- leading civil rights activists and African American leaders
- black political movements within the USA
- crucial legal and political developments
- the portrayal of African Americans in popular culture.

*Black Civil Rights in America* is a concise survey which places the civil rights movement in the wider context of American history. It provides a lucid introduction to the very latest scholarship in African American history.

**Kevern Verney** is a Senior Lecturer in American History at Edge Hill College of Higher Education.

Introductions to History
This series of introductions to widely studied and newer areas of the undergraduate history curriculum provides short, clear, self-contained and incisive guides for the student reader.

## Introductions to History

Series Editor: David Birmingham,
*Professor of Modern History, University of Kent at Canterbury*

A series initiated by members of the School of History at the University of
Kent at Canterbury

# Black Civil Rights in America

Kevern Verney

*Edge Hill College of Higher Education*

London and New York

First published 2000
by Routledge
11 New Fetter Lane, London EC4P 4EE

Simultaneously published in the USA and Canada
by Routledge
29 West 35th Street, New York, NY 10001

*Routledge is an imprint of the Taylor & Francis Group*

© 2000 Kevern Verney

Typeset in Sabon and Gills Sans by Keystroke,
Jacaranda Lodge, Wolverhampton
Printed and bound in Great Britain by TJ International,
Padstow, Cornwall

*British Library Cataloguing in Publication Data*
A catalogue record for this book is available from the British Library

*Library of Congress Cataloging in Publication Data*
Verney, Kevern, 1960–
    Black civil rights in America / Kevern Verney.
        p.  cm.
    Includes bibliographical references (p. ) and index.
    ISBN 0-415-23887-0 (hb) – ISBN 0-415-23888-9 (pb)
    1. Afro-Americans–Civil rights–History–20th century. 2. Civil rights
movements–United States–History–20th century. 3. Afro-Americans–
Civil rights–History–19th century. 4. Civil rights movements–United
States–History–19th century. 5. United States–Race relations. I. Title.
E185.61 .V475 2000
323.1'196073–dc21                                                00-028066

ISBN 0–415–23887–0 (hbk)
ISBN 0–415–23888–9 (pbk)

# Contents

# Emancipation and accommodation

Black slaves first arrived in the British colonies of North America in 1619 at Jamestown, Virginia. During the War of Independence, 1776–83, slavery was abolished in the middle and northern colonies, or states, as they had by then become. The 1776 Declaration of Independence, drafted by Thomas Jefferson, moreover affirmed that all men were created equal, 'endowed by their creator with certain inalienable rights', and that among these were the rights to 'life, liberty and the pursuit of happiness'. Despite this seeming promise of freedom, black slavery continued in the southern states of America. Slaves were the principal labour-force in the cultivation of tobacco, sugar and above all cotton, production of which greatly expanded following the invention of the cotton gin by Eli Whitney in 1793. Although the legal importation of slaves was banned in 1808, a substantial illicit influx of African slaves continued. More significantly, slave numbers within the United States grew by natural population increase and by 1860 there were some 4 million slaves in the South.

Geographically, slavery expanded westwards in the early decades of the nineteenth century. In a major interregional migration younger generations of planters from the South Atlantic states (Delaware, Maryland, Virginia, North and South Carolina, Georgia and Florida) moved to the fertile cotton-growing territories of the Deep South (Texas, Louisiana, Mississippi and Alabama).

In the North mounting opposition to slavery, or the 'Peculiar Institution', as it was known, led to the founding of the anti-slavery journal *The Liberator* by William Lloyd Garrison in Massachusetts in 1831. This marked the start of the radical abolitionist movement.

Sectional North–South tensions over slavery increased during the 1840s and the 1850s. Reasons for northern hostility were many and complex. The westward expansion of slave labour was seen as unfair economic competition for free settlers. There was anxiety over the political strength of the southern planter aristocracy, the 'Slave Power', at both national and state level. Although there was concern at the inhumanity of slavery, few thought that African Americans should ever have the right to full citizenship. Opponents of slavery more often believed that emancipation should be followed by the colonization of freed slaves out of the United States to Africa or the Caribbean. Within the northern states free blacks were routinely denied the right to vote and subject to discrimination in employment and social life.

The immediate cause of the American Civil War of 1861–5 was not a northern attempt to abolish slavery but the refusal of the North to accept the right of southern states to secede, or withdraw, from the Union. During his 1860 election campaign the new Republican president, Abraham Lincoln, pledged not to interfere with the institution of slavery. At the outbreak of war on 12 April 1861 five slave states, Delaware, Kentucky, Maryland, Missouri and West Virginia, chose to remain within the Union. In the early months of the conflict Union commanders in the field were instructed to return fugitive slaves to their owners, as to do otherwise was construed as a violation of property rights. It was not until the Emancipation Proclamation of 1 January 1863 that Lincoln finally committed the North to the abolition of slavery. This was confirmed by the passage of the thirteenth amendment to the US Constitution in 1865. The amendment was needed to end any doubts over the legality of Lincoln's action. It also provided for emancipation in slave states that had remained in the Union and which had been excluded from the 1863 proclamation.

Emancipation, when it came, was a result of military expediency rather than part of any carefully thought-out strategy. This had important long-term consequences. The thirteenth amendment told slaves what they were free from but not what they were free for. It was not until the Civil Rights Act of 1866 and the fourteenth and fifteenth amendments to the Constitution, ratified in 1869 and 1870 respectively, that blacks were given full citizenship and voting rights. Even then, the fourteenth amendment's requirement that no 'state shall deny any person within its jurisdiction the equal protection of the laws' did not ensure integrated equality. At the same time that the amendment was passed Congress authorized segregated black and white schooling in Washington, DC.

Little was done by the federal government to help slaves adapt to freedom. The Freedmen's Bureau, established in 1865, gave limited assistance and made school buildings available. Teachers were provided by charitable and philanthropic societies such as the American Missionary Association (AMA). The Bureau was chronically understaffed and lacking in resources. John De Forest, a Bureau agent in South Carolina, was given an area to administer two-thirds the size of Connecticut. The *laissez-faire* values of the late nineteenth century ensured that the Bureau provided little in the way of charitable aid lest it encouraged a culture of dependency. Although the Bureau lasted until 1872, most of its operations were effectively wound up by 1869. Moreover, the Bureau had to be renewed on a year-by-year basis, encouraging a permanent philosophy of short-termism.

Contrary to the prevailing popular myth that ex-slaves would be given 'forty acres and a mule', federal and state authorities provided blacks with no land or money to safeguard their economic independence. Despite this there were some striking examples of black economic success, most notably among land cooperatives of ex-slaves in the Sea Islands of Georgia and South Carolina and the all-black Davis Bend community in Mississippi, led by a former slave Benjamin Montgomery.

Overall the picture was more depressing. Lacking capital and resources, most freedmen were forced to enter into labour agreements with their former masters or other planters in their locality. Sharecropping became the most common form of agriculture in the South after 1865 and continued in widespread use until the 1930s. Under this system black families were provided with plots of land by white landowners to work on their own as small independent farmers. At harvest time the planter was repaid with a one-third to one-half share of the crop. On the surface this appeared to be a fair market compromise between the aspirations of freed slaves and landowners. In reality the system reduced many blacks to a kind of neo-serfdom scarcely better than their former slave condition. Illiterate ex-slaves were cheated by one-sided contracts. They were compelled to buy overpriced goods and provisions from plantation stores. This combined with extortionate rates of interest meant that come the harvest, planters often claimed 100 per cent or more of the annual cotton crop. In following years sharecropper families were forced into mere subsistence farming in a vain attempt to pay off ever-mounting debts.

During the Reconstruction era, 1865–77, national political life was dominated by the Republican Party, which had uninterrupted control of Congress and the presidency. On 14 April 1865 Abraham Lincoln was assassinated by a southern extremist, John Wilkes Booth. He was succeeded by Vice-President Andrew Johnson. Johnson, a southerner and racial conservative, sought to broker a lenient peace for the defeated South. This brought him into conflict with more radical Republicans in Congress led by Charles Sumner and Thaddeus Stevens. Johnson vetoed all reconstruction legislation passed by Congress and in 1867 was impeached for failing to oversee faithfully the execution of the laws of the land. In a trial before the United States Senate he narrowly avoided being removed from office.

The years 1867–77 were a high point for congressional or 'Radical' reconstruction. In the election of 1868 Johnson was succeeded as President by the northern war hero Ulysses S. Grant. Re-elected in 1872, Grant enjoyed good relations with Congress.

At local level the Republican Party secured control of state governments in the South for the first time during Reconstruction. These Republican administrations were maintained in power by a voting coalition of blacks, northern newcomers to the South – the 'Carpetbaggers' – and a minority of white southerners – the 'Scalawags'. In popular mythology Republican governments in the South have been portrayed as greedy and corrupt, leading to oppressive taxation of the impoverished white South. In fact, high taxes resulted more from the costs of rebuilding after the Civil War and the long overdue modernization of southern society, for example the introduction of public schools. Although there was some fraud and dishonesty, this was greatly exaggerated by opposition southern Democrats for political gain. This culminated in a popular crusade against tyranny and corruption, the so-called 'Redemption' period of 1875–7. In these years white Democrats regained political control of the South by the systematic use of electoral fraud, violence and intimidation. Black voters, dependent for their livelihood on whites, were subject to wholesale economic coercion. In the 1880s the white planter class or 'Bourbon' aristocracy enjoyed political power across the South.

This supremacy was briefly threatened in the 1890s by the emergence of the People's Party, an alliance of poor white farmers and black sharecroppers. By the late 1890s the challenge posed by the People's Party, or 'Populists', as they were generally known, had collapsed. Persistent racial enmity and the entrenched power of the planter class proved too difficult to overcome. In the wake of the Populist movement state governments in the South sought to exclude blacks from political life altogether. New laws were introduced that required applicants for voter registration to pass literacy tests, or demonstrate an understanding of selected passages from state constitutions. In *Williams* v. *Mississippi*, 1898, the US Supreme Court ruled that such measures were constitutional. The rights of blacks under the fourteenth and fifteenth amendments were not deemed have been violated because the new laws made no specific reference to race. Within a few years the large majority of blacks in the South were, by these indirect means, denied all voting rights. Black disenfranchisement persisted largely unchecked until the 1960s.

In another landmark decision, *Plessy* v. *Ferguson*, 1896, the Supreme Court accepted the constitutionality of racial segregation. In an 8–1 majority ruling the justices on the court developed the concept of 'separate but equal'. Separate facilities for whites and blacks were held not to violate black citizenship rights because separation in itself did not imply superior or inferior treatment for either race. Racial segregation under the law rapidly spread throughout the South and extended to most aspects of life. Seating in theatres, restaurants and public transport, schools, hospitals, the workplace, restrooms and even cemeteries was affected. Facilities provided for blacks were usually grossly inferior. Despite this the 'separate but equal' ruling was not overturned by the Supreme Court until the case of *Brown* v. *the Topeka Board of Education* in 1954.

The origins of racial segregation, or 'Jim Crowism', as it came to be known, have been the subject of much historical controversy. In *The Strange Career of Jim Crow* (1955), written in the wake of the Brown case, the historian C. Vann Woodward argued that the segregation laws of the 1890s marked a major departure from earlier southern custom and tradition. Prior to this, blacks in the region had suffered from extreme discrimination, but there had not been a physical separation of the races. Other historians, most notably

Joel Williamson, contested this view. They claimed that separation under the law, *de jure* segregation, may have been new in the 1890s but separation in practice, *de facto* segregation, was commonplace by the late 1860s and early 1870s. The evidence on both sides in this debate is complicated by the fact that segregation may have developed earlier in the South Atlantic states and rural districts than in the Deep South or urban areas. Patterns of segregation were also confusing and inconsistent. In the late 1860s it was common for white and black children to play together yet still attend separate schools.

The most important African American leader of the nineteenth century was Frederick Douglass. Born in 1817, as a slave in Maryland, Douglass escaped to freedom in 1838. In the 1840s and 1850s he became a prominent member of the abolitionist movement and wrote an account of his earlier experiences, *The Narrative of the Life of an American Slave* (1845). More than just a racial spokesman, Douglass championed other radical causes of his day, including the emancipation of women and the rights of workers. During the Civil War and Reconstruction he was a loyal member of the Republican Party and a vigorous advocate of emancipation and full civil and political rights for blacks. In the 1880s and 1890s advancing age and the deteriorating conditions suffered by blacks led to Douglass toning down some of his former militancy. Nonetheless, he remained a strong defender of black civil rights to the end of his life in 1895.

The leadership vacuum created by the death of Douglass was filled by Booker T. Washington. Born around 1856 in Virginia, Washington was the last great African American leader to experience slavery directly. From 1872 to 1875 he was educated at the Hampton Institute of Samuel Armstrong in Virginia. In 1881 Washington became Principal of his own college, Tuskegee Institute in Alabama. Starting with virtually no resources Washington developed Tuskegee into the best-known black educational institution in the South.

Armstrong and his disciple Washington supported the idea of industrial education. Popular at the time, this stressed the need to teach working-class and black children practical vocational skills, such as woodwork, rather than more academic subjects like music or literature. In part this was a reaction to the kind of tuition that had been provided for blacks during the Civil War and Reconstruction. Northern missionary educators in the South had stressed religious education and the teaching of subjects like algebra, rather than catering to the more immediate practical needs of illiterate ex-slaves. Advocates of industrial education also sought to break down the deep hostility of southern whites to any form of schooling for blacks. Former slaves would not be educated above their ability, or given unrealistic social expectations, but would rather be trained for agricultural labour and domestic service.

In 1895 Washington achieved national recognition as a result of his 'Atlanta Compromise' speech at an international cotton exposition in that city. An accommodationist, Washington acknowledged the reality of worsening racial conditions. Publicly, he accepted the inevitability of segregation, arguing that whites and blacks could be 'as separate as the fingers' in 'all things that are purely social' but 'one as the hand in all things essential to mutual progress'. Washington urged blacks to concentrate first on education and economic self-help rather than agitate for political and civil rights. From 1895 to his death in 1915 Washington was the dominant black spokesman in the United States. He was an unofficial adviser to two presidents, Theodore Roosevelt, 1901–9, and William Taft, 1909–13. Washington's autobiography, *Up From Slavery* (1901), received widespread acclaim, both in the United States and Europe, and he achieved international recognition as an educator and race leader.

Despite his success Washington was a controversial figure with many black opponents, particularly in the North. In their newspaper the *Boston Guardian* William Monroe Trotter and George Washington Forbes regularly attacked Washington as too conservative and deferential to white opinion. Washington's most thoughtful and persuasive critic was the black intellectual W. E. B. DuBois. In a famous essay, 'Of Mr Booker T. Washington and Others', published in his book *The Souls of Black Folk* (1903), DuBois engaged in a considered appraisal of Washington's philosophy. He argued that stress on industrial education overlooked the need for higher learning. This failing, combined with neglect of civil and political rights, meant that Washington's programme was effectively preparing blacks for second-class citizenship. In 1905 DuBois formed the Niagara Movement, a small organization composed mainly of black intellectuals, to oppose Washington's leadership. This met with little success, partly because of Washington's attempts to sabotage the group. The organization also suffered from elitism, reflecting DuBois's belief in the need for racial leadership to be provided by the 'talented tenth', a select core of educated and professional blacks.

In 1909 DuBois became a founder member of the new biracial National Association for the Advancement of Colored People (NAACP). Although DuBois was appointed editor of the NAACP journal *Crisis*, leadership of the organization was dominated by white liberals in its early years. These included the social reformer Mary White Ovington, journalist William Walling and leading lawyer Morefield Storey. Often white members came from an abolitionist background, such as New York newspaper editor Oswald Garrison Villard, a grandson of William Lloyd Garrison.

In the last years of his life Washington's leadership was challenged increasingly by the NAACP. Washington himself became less accommodationist. He attacked the excesses of imperialism abroad and became more outspoken in his criticism of segregation at home.

Eulogized by leading whites of his day, Washington's conservative philosophy has made him an unattractive figure to modern historians. His reputation was partially rehabilitated in the work of his most recent and scholarly biographer, Louis Harlan. Harlan focused attention on Washington's so-called 'secret life'. Deferential in his public statements, Washington engaged in a variety of covert civil rights activities, sponsoring anti-segregation lawsuits and writing anonymous critical editorials in black newspapers. Less appealingly, he covertly sabotaged the efforts of his black critics. Dissenting groups were silenced by infiltration of their meetings, malicious lawsuits and other underhand tactics. Conversely, the 'Tuskegee machine' secured patronage and career advancement for Washington's supporters.

Negative white attitudes towards blacks at the end of the nineteenth century were reflected in the popular culture of the period. In the 1870s and 1880s white audiences were entertained by travelling 'Tom Troops' enacting scenes from Harriet Beecher Stowe's abolitionist novel, *Uncle Tom's Cabin* (1851). Minstrel shows with African American entertainers, and whites made up in burnt cork to mimic black characters, were also common. First popular in the North during the 1830s, minstrel shows enjoyed a rebirth of popularity in the 1880s and 1890s. In 1880 the southern white journalist Joel Chandler Harris published the Brer Rabbit folklore of former slaves in *The Songs and Sayings of Uncle Remus*.

These popular representations of blacks were all deeply racist. African Americans were typically shown as childish, incompetent, and dependent on white guidance. At the same time there were some 'benign' aspects in this racial stereotyping, with blacks also depicted as kind, loyal and well-meaning.

In the early years of the twentieth century more sinister imagery began to emerge. In popular novels like Thomas Dixon's *The Leopard's Spots* (1902) and *The Clansman* (1905), blacks were depicted as savage with animal-like traits. Black men became menacing figures who threatened to defile southern white womanhood. This portrayal reflected the myth of the black rapist that was common in southern society around 1900. On the flimsiest of evidence alleged black rapists were put to death in a horrifying manner by white lynch mobs. Between 1889 and 1899 there were an average of 188 lynchings a year in the United States. The large majority of these were in the South and racially motivated.

Such was the success of Dixon's works that in 1915 *The Clansman* was used as the basis for D. W. Griffiths's film *Birth of a Nation*. Telling the story of two families during the Civil War and Reconstruction, the film was a milestone in cinema history and the first box-office blockbuster. It was also one of the most racist films ever made by Hollywood. Dixon's racial stereotypes were faithfully adapted to the silver screen. The Reconstruction era was portrayed as a national disaster, a time when freed black slaves were given civil and political rights that they were unfit to exercise.

Ironically, the Hollywood view of history was for once supported by historical scholars of the day, most notably in the works of William Dunning and his school of Reconstruction historians at Columbia University from 1886 to 1922. At the same time pseudo-scientific studies, by researchers such as Carl Brigham, Luther Burbank, Henry Osburn and Henry Suksdorf, sought to prove black racial inferiority.

Within African American communities, segregation, and the rural isolation of many parts of the South, meant that blacks were largely excluded from many aspects of white society. This resulted in the development of distinctive black cultural forms and institutions. Before 1865 black slaves kept African cultural traditions alive in their music, dance and folklore. This enabled blacks to resist the psychological oppression of slavery by maintaining their own communal identity. The social exclusion of blacks after the Civil

9

War helped to ensure the continued survival of syncretic, but still African-influenced, cultural patterns. Black culture also mirrored the experiences and suffering of ex-slaves themselves. After 1865 the labour gangs of slavery gave way to the more individualistic system of sharecropping. Marking this change, by the early 1900s the traditional ballads and work hollers of slave field hands evolved into the highly personalized and melancholy Blues. The advent of the Blues equally reflected the new urban living conditions experienced by growing numbers of blacks and technological advances in the commercial recording of music.

In a different vein, the exclusion of blacks from white theatres and dance halls highlighted the need for cheap and accessible entertainment at black social gatherings. This contributed to the emergence of Ragtime in the 1880s and 1890s. In 1899 the *Maple Leaf Rag* by 'King of Ragtime' Scott Joplin transcended the racial divide. Joplin's piano rags enjoyed national and international public acclaim. In an irony that was to be often repeated in the twentieth century, white audiences lionized the artistic creations of black culture whilst at the same time condemning blacks themselves to second-class citizenship.

# CHAPTER ONE

# New directions

## Urbanization and the Great Migration, 1915–30

American society experienced great change in the years 1880 to 1920. Rapid industrialization, mainly in the northern states, led to major urban growth. The population of New York City rose from 1.2 million in 1880 to 5.6 million by 1920. During this period the population of Chicago, a gateway to the West and a centre of the meatpacking industry, increased from just over half a million to 2.7 million. In the same years, Detroit, which became a key location for automobile production, saw a rise in population from 16,360 to just under 1 million, and the population of Pittsburgh, home of the steel industry, grew from 235,071 to 588,343.

Expansion was partly sustained by internal migration from farming communities in the West. In the last decades of the nineteenth century small farmers experienced economic hardship, the result of falling prices, high interest rates and heavy transport costs. Financial difficulties combined with the lure of city life led to a population decline in many rural areas.

The most important source of urban growth was overseas immigration, particularly from southern and eastern European countries like Russia, Poland, Greece and Italy. Between 1880 and 1921 over 23.5 million immigrants arrived in the United States. The influx peaked in the early years of the twentieth century, with 8.8 million immigrants arriving between 1901 and 1910, and over 1.2 million in 1914 alone.

Before the First World War blacks were comparatively unaffected by economic change. At the turn of the century at least 90 per cent of African Americans still lived in the South. Some southern cities, such as Richmond in Virginia, Atlanta in Georgia and Birmingham in Alabama, experienced significant growth between 1880 and 1920, but the region as a whole remained mostly rural. Cotton production, sustained by the sharecropping system, continued to be the mainstay of the southern economy. Moreover, blacks seeking to escape debt peonage in the South by migration to the North encountered formidable problems. Leaving meant separation from family, friends and home surroundings. In the North, racial prejudice made it difficult for blacks to compete for jobs against European immigrants. African Americans were frequently excluded from trade union membership. Accommodation was expensive and hard to find. For these reasons most blacks preferred to put up with the life they already knew rather than seek opportunities elsewhere.

The situation changed dramatically with the outbreak of the First World War. From 1915 European immigration to the United States fell sharply, initially as a result of wartime conditions and later because of legal restrictions induced by postwar xenophobia. At the same time industrial growth continued and even increased because of new wartime production. Northern employers countered the loss of immigrant labour by actively recruiting African Americans instead. Between 1915 and 1925 this led to the 'Great Migration' as 1.25 million blacks left the South to take up employment in the North. Most migrants settled in a small number of leading urban centres. From 1910 to 1930 the black population of Chicago rose from 44,103 to 233,903, and that of New York from 91,709 to 327,706. Cleveland, Detroit, Indianapolis, Philadelphia and Pittsburgh also saw a large increase in their African American communities. Explanations for the migration have traditionally centred on 'push-pull' analysis; the negative or 'push' features of the South encouraged blacks to leave the region, and the positive or 'pull' features of the North made it attractive to migrants.

Blacks were repelled from the South for a variety of reasons. Economic deprivation of black sharecroppers was made worse by strictly enforced social subordination to whites in most aspects of day-to-day life. Minor breaches of racial etiquette resulted in blacks losing their employment, home or worse. Between 1900 and 1909 at least 754 African Americans were lynched in the United States, with 92 per cent of lynchings taking place in the South. On average at least 60 blacks a year were lynched in the southern states between 1900 and 1914. Some victims stood accused of rape or other serious crimes, but others were killed for minor offences that breached social conventions rather than legal norms. The publicly tolerated murder of blacks by white vigilante mobs, lynchings were frequently horrific public spectacles in which the hapless victims were subjected to torture and barbarity of medieval dimensions. This included castration, disembowelling and being burnt alive. The number of lynchings actually dropped at the start of the twentieth century, after a peak of over 100 a year between 1880 and 1900. However, this modest improvement was sufficient to persuade only the most optimistic of blacks, such as Booker T. Washington, that race relations were starting to get better. In particular, younger generations of southern blacks, with no direct experience of slavery, were less willing than their parents and grandparents to tolerate conditions in the South.

A desire to leave was reinforced by worsening economic conditions as cotton crops were decimated by a new insect pest, the boll weevil. First arriving in Texas from Mexico in 1892, the weevil gradually moved eastwards, reaching Georgia and the Carolinas by the early 1920s. In any given year up to 50 per cent of cotton crops could be destroyed by the pest, and weevil damage from 1892 to 1918 was estimated to cost $250 million, a loss of some 4.5 million bales of cotton. Sharecroppers, who even in good times were the most marginal of cotton producers, were usually the first to suffer.

At the same time as the boll weevil ruined livelihoods in the South, a wartime boom in industrial output created unprecedented job opportunities for blacks in the North. During the First World War northern factory workers could earn from $2.25 to $3.25 per day, compared to only 75 cents a day for farm labourers in the South. This economic pull was reinforced by better social conditions. Migrants often wrote letters home praising high wages and more liberal race relations in the North. Initial migrant groups thus encouraged further waves of migration and provided reception areas for later newcomers.

Although racism was ever present in the North, and intensified as a result of black migration, conditions were still notably better than in the South. Blacks in the North were able to enjoy voting rights and could hope to provide a better education and future for their children. Black newspapers, most notably the influential *Chicago Defender*, run by Tuskegee graduate Robert Abbott, highlighted opportunities in the North. The *Defender* was widely circulated in the South and even banned by some southern states.

The experience of black migrants once in the North has been the subject of much debate. Better wage levels were offset by higher living costs and expensive, overcrowded accommodation. In terms of health and social welfare, migrants often exchanged one set of problems for another. Deficiency diseases and racial brutality in the South were replaced by tuberculosis, juvenile delinquency and high ghetto crime rates in the North. Despite this, few migrants chose to return to the South.

It used to be accepted by historians that migrants experienced a limited, but clear, improvement in their quality of life. More recent accounts by scholars such as Carole Marks have been less positive. Northern industrial employers, able to take advantage of cheap non-unionized labour, were the real short-term beneficiaries of the Great Migration rather than black migrants themselves.

Black migrants also tended to fare badly in comparison to European immigrants. The latest newcomers to city life, African Americans lagged behind other ethnic groups in political and labour organization. Most black workers remained non-unionized until the 1930s. African Americans were less successful than other ethnic groups in gaining patronage and a share of the spoils system operated by urban political party machines. Moreover, although other minority communities like the Irish, Italians, Jews and Slavs suffered from bigotry, the problem was worse for African Americans. The children of immigrants could, by changing their names and adopting American-style dress and customs, hope to escape prejudice. Permanent differences in physical appearance meant that racism was a burden inherited by successive generations of African Americans.

The fact that black migrants were already American citizens and the fact that they were fluent in English gave them only limited advantage over immigrants. Socially, the rural South, although a part of the United States, was in many respects as far removed from the likes of New York and Chicago as peasant communities in Europe. Language difficulties reinforced group solidarity in immigrant neighbourhoods, encouraging the development of ethnic businesses and social institutions. African American migrants, by comparison, were less successful in developing autonomous community organizations, in part because they did not experience the same linguistic barriers.

The Great Migration had a profound impact on African American life. The ghettos of the North became home to a talented young generation of black artists and intellectuals in a cultural flowering known as the Harlem Renaissance. Black writers such as Langston Hughes, Claude McKay and Jean Toomer achieved literary fame. Although often sharply critical of US race relations, their works acquired cult status among fashionable white middle-class readers.

In popular music, Blues and Ragtime fused with brass band and dance music to produce the new phenomenon of Jazz. Black musicians and singers such as Duke Ellington, Adelaide Hall and Cab Calloway became national celebrities. The Cotton Club in Harlem, featuring all-black cabaret shows, became a centre of New York nightlife. Black musicals such as *Shuffle Along* (1922), *Chocolate Dandies* (1923) and *Blackbirds* (1926–8) played to packed houses on Broadway. Another African American revue, *Runnin' Wild* (1923), introduced the Charleston as the new dance craze of the decade. The following year Paul Robeson played the leading role in Eugene O'Neill's *All God's Chillun Got Wings*. The production not only launched Robeson's international career, but was the first time that a black man played the principal role opposite a white actress in a Broadway performance. Some artists, like Robeson, believed that the richness and diversity of black cultural achievement would help to break down barriers of racial prejudice and bigotry.

Ironically, the social impact of the Great Migration had the opposite effect. Most large cities of the North had small African American communities before the First World War. These 'old settlers' were relatively few and, if subject to racial discrimination, did not generally suffer from institutionalized segregation – the culturally or legally enforced separation of the races. The influx of the 'new settlers' after 1915 greatly increased the visibility of African American communities. Racial tensions increased and formal segregation spread to many northern cities for the first time. 'Old settlers' often blamed the newcomers for worsening conditions and perceived them as backward and unsophisticated. Black residential areas, such as Harlem in New York and the South Side in Chicago, became overcrowded, forcing up rents and creating a shortage of living accommodation. Often large families were forced to live in squalid single-room 'kitchenette' apartments with only the most basic facilities. When black ghettos began to expand into neighbouring white residential areas, racial violence frequently resulted. Tensions increased at the end of the First World War in 1918 as both black and white soldiers returned home and were placed in competition for employment. During the 'Red Summer' of 1919 there were over 25 race riots in cities across the United States. The worst disorder was in Chicago during July, when 15 whites and 23 blacks were killed, 520 people injured and over 1,000 African American families made homeless as black houses were burnt by white mobs.

The end of the war saw not only a worsening of race relations but a reawakening of conservative values in America. In a reaction to the horrors of the war in Europe the United States retreated into isolationism, declining to join the newly created international peacekeeping organization, the League of Nations, in 1919–20. Nativist fears of foreign influences, especially political and labour radicalism, culminated in the 1924 National Origins Act. This limited total immigration to the United States to only 165,000 persons in any year, and that mostly from the perceived Nordic and Anglo-Saxon countries of northern and western Europe. Southern and western states in the United States experienced a revival of religious fundamentalism. In a vain attempt to regain lost innocence the whole nation was pledged to abstinence from alcohol by the introduction of Prohibition with the passage of the eighteenth amendment to the US Constitution in 1919.

Although immigration controls helped to ensure continued job opportunities for black migrants, the 'New Era' of conservatism generally made life more difficult for African Americans. A striking example of this was the re-emergence of the Ku Klux Klan. First formed in Pulaski, Tennessee, in 1866, the original Klan expanded to some 500,000 members and terrorized blacks and Republican voters throughout the South in the late 1860s and early 1870s. Ultimately suppressed by the federal authorities, the organization was effectively defunct by 1872.

In 1915 a new Klan was formed in Atlanta, Georgia, by a defrocked Methodist minister, William Joseph Simmons. The revival was prompted by the murder of a local white girl, Mary Phagan, and because of the glamorous portrayal of the Klan in the film *Birth of a Nation*. Over the next ten years Klan membership rapidly expanded, reaching 100,000 in 1921 and 4 million by 1924. Full-time Klan agents known as Kleagles used aggressive marketing techniques to recruit new members, not just in the South but throughout the nation. The Klan succeeded by appealing to a combination of commonly held fears and prejudices – racism, xenophobia, anti-semitism, anti-

Catholicism and anti-communism. In cities like Chicago the Klan recruited strongly in 'zones of emergence' – white residential areas adjoining black or immigrant ghettos. After 1925 Klan membership sharply declined, falling to just 45,000 by 1930. This was largely because of changing public perceptions of the Klan following shocking revelations about corruption and criminality in the organization. However, the racial conservatism that supported the initial rise of the Klan remained.

Under these conditions liberal whites and African Americans found it difficult to achieve any improvements in race relations. In 1911 the National Urban League (NUL) was founded out of two earlier organizations, the National League for the Protection of Colored Women and the Committee for Improving the Industrial Conditions of Negroes in New York. The most conservative of the major civil rights organizations in the twentieth century, the Urban League was initially dominated by wealthy and middle-class white philanthropists. It was created to provide practical help and advice to urban black communities rather than to campaign actively for social and political reform.

The NAACP was, by comparison, more radical in its outlook. Its main efforts were concentrated on a legalistic strategy of challenging segregation and discrimination in the courts. This approach led to only limited gains before the 1930s. A rare breakthrough came in 1917 when, in *Buchanan* v. *Warley*, the US Supreme Court held that city ordinances enforcing residential segregation were unconstitutional. Victory was even then less than complete. The ruling of the judges derived less from concerns over racial fairness than the belief that such laws violated the property rights of homeowners.

From 1909 to 1934 the NAACP journal *Crisis* was edited by W. E. B. DuBois, and in 1920 another African American, James Weldon Johnson, was appointed as NAACP Executive Secretary. The organization began to develop grassroots black support with 274 branches or chapters and over 90,000 members by the early 1920s. Despite these advances the NAACP did not achieve a truly mass membership until the 1940s. It continued to be perceived as an elitist and largely white-run organization until the late 1920s.

One of the few positive developments to result from the Red Summer of race riots was the founding in 1919 of the Commission on Interracial Cooperation (CIC) in Atlanta, Georgia. The Commission was set up by southern white liberals with the support of a few

African American spokespersons to campaign for interracial dialogue and understanding. Between 1919 and 1943 it sponsored academic studies on southern race relations and supported black education with the aid of grants from the Julius Rosenwald Fund, a charitable offshoot of the business giant Sears Roebuck.

The death of Booker T. Washington in November 1915 marked a turning point in terms of African American leadership. Robert Russa Moton, Washington's successor as Principal of Tuskegee, was an able educator but with no aspiration to be a national race leader. Washington's leading black critics, such as W. E. B. DuBois and William Monroe Trotter, lacked charisma and genuine mass appeal. The leadership vacuum left by Washington was filled not by any established African American spokesperson but by Marcus Garvey, a newcomer to the United States from the West Indies.

Born in 1887, Garvey spent the first 23 years of his life in Jamaica. Between 1910 and 1914 he travelled widely in Central and South America and Europe, settling in London. Inspired by Booker T. Washington's autobiography, *Up From Slavery* (1901), he returned to Jamaica in 1914 and established the Universal Negro Improvement Association (UNIA). The UNIA was initially intended to promote industrial education as practised by Washington at Tuskegee. Short of money, Garvey landed in New York in 1916 to embark on a fund-raising tour of the United States. A forceful and energetic speaker, he soon began to gain recognition and respect in African American society. In 1917 he formed a branch of the UNIA in Harlem, New York and within a year recruited some 1,000 members. During 1918 he established a weekly newspaper, *The Negro World*, which achieved a wide circulation first in the United States and later in the Caribbean, South America and Africa.

In 1919 Garvey began a series of UNIA economic initiatives. The Negro Factories Corporation (NFC) was set up to promote black-run businesses and founded a chain of retail outlets. Between 1919 and 1921 a more ambitious project, the Black Star Line (BSL), sought to launch an international black steamship company, buying three ships, the SS *Yarmouth*, the SS *Kanawha* and the *Shadyside*. The money for these purchases was raised by the sale of $750,000 of share certificates to thousands of small black investors. Garvey hoped that the BSL, which was started as a business venture, would help fulfil his wider vision of uniting black peoples worldwide in international commerce.

By this time he had moved away from Booker T. Washington's integrationist philosophy. Garvey was now a black nationalist who rejected the view that blacks could ever be fully assimilated as equals into US society. Instead African Americans should develop their own institutions and minimize contacts with whites. Ultimately, Garvey hoped to achieve an end to European colonialism in Africa and the Caribbean and to create an independent black African state. In August 1920 delegates from over 25 countries attended the UNIA First International Convention of the Negro Peoples of the World held in Harlem. The Convention elected Garvey as Provisional President of the anticipated new African republic and adopted its own red, green and white flag and a national anthem, 'Ethiopia, Thou Land of our Fathers'. Garvey created a black nobility, the 'Knights of the Nile', and began to develop a national organizational infrastructure in-waiting with the formation of groups like the African Legion, the Garvey Militia, the Black Eagle Flying Corps and the Universal African Motor Corps. This reflected the fact that Garvey believed that the leadership roles in the new republic would be filled by black Americans selected to join a 'Back to Africa' programme.

At its peak in 1923 the UNIA had a membership of over 1 million in the United States alone, as well as 120,000 members in Central and Southern America and 30,000 members in Africa. There were a variety of reasons for this remarkable success. Garvey himself was a charismatic orator. He appealed to African American audiences by urging them to take a pride in their own history, culture and racial ancestry. Garvey's African Orthodox Church, established under Chaplain-General George Alexander McGuire, provided images of a black God and a black Christ.

In addition to a sense of racial self-worth Garvey's economic initiatives offered blacks the prospect of practical self-help. UNIA Liberty Halls in northern cities served as local community centres, dispensing advice, free food and temporary accommodation and providing a venue for social functions. UNIA members could hope for employment in an NFC business. Purchasers of BSL shares anticipated future dividends as well as racial pride in return for their investments.

Garveyism was particularly popular in the expanding ghettos of the North. The emergence of large semi-autonomous black communities in cities like Chicago and New York made his ideas of racial separatism appear realistic. The UNIA actively recruited new southern migrants. This was in contrast to established black middle-class community leaders, who were often elitist and patronizing in their attitudes to the newcomers.

In New York, the effective headquarters of the Garvey movement, the UNIA benefited from the presence of a sizable West Indian community. In the 1920s at least 16–17 per cent of the black population of the city, or over 54,000 people, were foreign born, and most of these were of West Indian origin. Generally better educated and more assertive of their civil rights than native black Americans, West Indian immigrants were an important potential source of grassroots leadership. Moreover, West Indians had a particular reputation for success in business, and for this reason were nicknamed the 'Jews of their race'.

In the wider world Garvey's calls for an end to colonialism were attractive to many young blacks in Africa and the Third World. The mutual fratricidal destruction of leading European colonial powers during the First World War also created hopes that the age of imperialism was approaching an end.

The contribution and achievements of Garvey as a race leader have been the subject of much controversy. By 1922 the Black Star Line was in a state of economic ruin with virtually no realizable assets, following a series of poor investments and disastrous commercial undertakings. In 1925 Garvey himself was convicted of fraud for continuing to advertise shares in the line. Jailed for two years, he was released in 1927 and deported. Following his departure the UNIA in the United States went into a steep decline. Settling first in Jamaica, and then in England, Garvey never succeeded in fulfilling his vision of an independent black African republic. He died in London in 1940, a largely forgotten figure.

Between 1920 and 1924 W. E. B. DuBois wrote a series of articles in *Crisis* that were highly critical of Garvey. These accused him of promoting fanciful and grandiose schemes to attract investments from poor blacks who could ill afford to engage in such speculation. Garvey's 'Back to Africa' project was singled out for particular criticism as crude and unrealistic. DuBois was irritated that this venture was often confused with his own more sophisticated Pan-African philosophy. Like Garvey, DuBois supported the goal of decolonization and believed that black Americans should strongly identify with their ancestral heritage in Africa. However, this should take the form of a spiritual rediscovery of African culture and values rather than simplistic notions of a physical migration back to the Dark Continent.

DuBois also believed that Garvey was seeking to instil inappropriate West Indian values and attitudes in black American society. In Jamaica racial divisions took different forms from in the United States. Whites comprised only about 2 per cent of the inhabitants of the island. A black labouring class made up 80 per cent of the population. In between these two groups was a mixed-race caste, accounting for some 18 per cent of the island's residents. This middle group aspired to acceptance and inclusion within the white community, and tended to look down on the majority black population as social inferiors. Coming from this background Garvey displayed a consistent distrust of blacks of mixed-race ancestry within the United States. He suspected light-skinned African Americans, like DuBois, of lacking racial loyalty and being motivated primarily by a desire for social recognition from whites.

In a wider context West Indian immigrants were often viewed with suspicion by native black Americans. They were perceived as foreign in their outlook and too much influenced by British colonial values, which were out of place in US society. On these grounds Garvey's efforts to establish a black aristocracy with his order of the 'Knights of the Nile' became an obvious target for criticism.

The perception of West Indians as outsiders was reinforced by their clannish nature and a tendency to be aloof and condescending in their social attitudes towards black Americans. Even the accepted West Indian business acumen could be a source of envy and tension as much as admiration. West Indians were seen as untrustworthy in their financial dealings and sometimes resented as a source of economic competition.

Some African American spokesmen, such as William Pickens of the NAACP and the rising labour leader Asa Philip Randolph, were initially prepared to give Garvey qualified backing. This support ended in 1922 when Garvey met with leaders of the Ku Klux Klan in an attempt to expand the UNIA's organization in the South, where the majority of black Americans still lived. Garvey justified this initiative as simply a realistic appraisal of race relations in America. Moreover, the UNIA and the Klan shared common beliefs in racial pride and racial separatism. These arguments failed to convince Garvey's critics. Almost all civil rights groups and race leaders denounced the UNIA president. In 1923 prominent African American spokespersons, including Pickens and Randolph, launched a 'Garvey must go' campaign to hasten his prosecution for fraud and deportation.

Later historians have been divided in their views on Garvey. Some, such as Garvey's first serious biographer, E. David Cronon, have seen him as a dangerous extremist, akin to Mussolini's fascist movement in Italy. Other commentators, including Theodore Vincent and Tony Martin, have been more positive. They perceive Garvey as ahead of his time: a visionary who inspired future independence movements in Africa and later black nationalist leaders in the United States, like Malcolm X. They argue that whilst Garvey's business initiatives may, sometimes, have been impractical, they gave black Americans a sense of dignity and self-worth. Similarly, failure of the UNIA in the United States and worldwide was as much the result of official persecution and the hostility of other black leaders as of Garvey's own shortcomings.

Viewed in an historical context the black nationalist philosophy of Garvey was part of a recurring phenomenon in the United States. Anti-slavery groups such as the American Colonization Society, founded in 1817, argued for black slaves to be returned to Africa well before the Civil War. Liberia, an independent African republic established in 1822 with US support, was seen as a natural homeland for black Americans.

Between the 1850s and the 1870s the black churchman Alexander Crummell and the black abolitionist leader Martin R. Delany both campaigned in separate projects to relocate freed slaves in Africa. During the 1880s and 1890s Henry McNeil Turner, a bishop in the African Methodist Episcopal Church, also promoted emigration to Africa. Later, from 1913 to 1915, the African-born Chief Sam tried unsuccessfully to establish a settlement of blacks from Oklahoma in the Gold Coast.

Within the United States itself two blacks, Henry Adams and 'Pap' Singleton, initiated the 'Exoduster' movement of 1879 in a failed internal migration of southern blacks to Kansas.

These various schemes, as well as being abortive, were all small-scale ventures. What made Garvey's UNIA movement unusual was not the originality of his ideas but its unprecedented popular appeal. Garvey was the first black nationalist leader to build up a mass organization and following in the United States. This achievement was a testimony to his unique abilities as a race leader. It was equally a measure of the despair of many black Americans over the state of US race relations.

CHAPTER TWO

# Seeds of change

The Great Depression and the Second World War,
1930–45

The Wall Street Crash of 1929 and the Great Depression that
followed had a profound impact on the lives of nearly all Americans.
Blacks suffered more than most. Economically insecure, and
with little in the way of savings, even during the comparative
prosperity of the 1920s, most African Americans were ill equipped
to meet the hardships of the 1930s. Racial discrimination added
to the suffering, with blacks typically being 'the last hired and
first fired'. By 1931 over 40 per cent of African Americans in
Pittsburgh were homeless and unemployed, and the situation
was similar in other leading cities. In 1932 30 per cent of blacks
in Chicago were out of work, 37 per cent in Detroit, 33 per cent in
Cleveland, 28 per cent in Philadelphia and 25 per cent in New York
City.

Despite chronic urban poverty and unemployment blacks
continued to migrate to the cities during the 1930s, albeit in smaller
numbers. From 1930 to 1939 some 400,000 African Americans left
the South for the urban North, compared to 800,000 in the decade
1920 to 1929. This population drift reflected the fact that if life in
the cities was hard, conditions in agriculture were even worse. The
Poindexter survey, a report on African American living conditions in
Alabama, Georgia and Mississippi from 1929 to 1937 commissioned
by the black Howard University in Washington, DC, revealed the
extent of the crisis. The study found that deficiency diseases like
anaemia, pellagra and rickets were rife among black agricultural
workers. Blacks made up some 47 per cent of the population in
the three states but accounted for 75–90 per cent of the identified
victims of hookworm, malaria and syphilis. Across the South as a

whole, as late as 1940 well over 70 per cent of black homes had neither electricity nor running water.

The administration of Republican President Herbert Hoover, 1929–33, did little to improve the situation. A *laissez-faire* conservative, Hoover believed that federal government aid to the poor and unemployed would distort natural market forces and create a culture of welfare dependency. Instead, those out of work should rely on self-help or 'rugged individualism'.

Hoover showed an equal lack of concern for black civil rights. Despite the fact that 57 blacks were lynched during his presidency, Hoover refused to condemn the actions of lynch mobs publicly. In 1930 he nominated a southern segregationist, John Parker of North Carolina, to fill a vacancy on the US Supreme Court. A vigorous lobbying campaign by the NAACP and trade union groups led to Parker's appointment being blocked by the US Senate. The victory was a testimony more to the power of organized labour than to the influence of civil rights groups. Nonetheless, it was a significant morale boost for the NAACP after its failed lobbying for a federal anti-lynching law, the Dyer bill, during the 1920s.

In the absence of concerted action by the Hoover administration blacks had to rely on their own initiative to alleviate the worst effects of the depression. Based in Harlem the black religious leader Father Divine (George Baker) turned to heavenly inspiration. Claiming to be the physical incarnation of God, Divine encouraged his followers to rely on positive thinking to counter economic hardship. On a practical level his community 'Peace Missions' established business cooperatives and restaurants to provide employment and cheap wholesome food. Despite his unorthodox religious views Father Divine gained over 2 million followers nationwide during the 1930s, including a niece of Herbert Hoover and the white Californian millionaire John Hunt or 'John the Revelator'. Peace Missions were established in leading cities across the United States, as well as overseas in Europe, Australia, Canada and the West Indies. The return of national prosperity in the early 1940s, combined with press revelations and internal scandals within the movement, led to a rapid decline of the Father Divine phenomenon. After Divine's death in 1965 a small Peace Mission movement continued to survive into the 1980s and 1990s under the leadership of his widow, Mother Divine.

The aims and objectives of the leading national black civil rights organization, the NAACP, were inevitably influenced by the Great

Depression. In 1930 James Weldon Johnson retired as NAACP Executive Secretary and was succeeded by another African American, Walter White. Under White the organization started to monitor black social and economic conditions more closely. In 1934–5 the internal Harris report advocated important shifts in NAACP strategy, including greater decentralization of power, more direct action campaigns and a stronger focus on economic issues in cooperation with trade union groups. Although never officially adopted by the NAACP Executive Board, the report's recommendations had an important influence on the organization's activities.

Less constructive were the growing personal and philosophical differences between Walter White and *Crisis* editor W. E. B. DuBois. By the early 1930s a growing admiration of Soviet communism had led to a radicalization of DuBois's ideas. At the same time DuBois believed that under White's conservative leadership the NAACP had failed to respond sufficiently to the economic suffering of blacks during the depression. In June 1934 DuBois resigned as *Crisis* editor and the following year outlined his own economic philosophy in a controversial article, 'A Negro Nation within a Nation'. Advocating a radical remedy for extreme conditions, he argued the case for racial self-segregation. African Americans should establish all-black economic cooperatives sustained by black consumers. This proposal was rejected outright by the NAACP leadership as incompatible with the organization's core commitment to integration. In fact this denunciation was based on an over-simple understanding of DuBois's views. His call for racial solidarity was made in response to the immediate economic crisis and did not rule out long-term interracial cooperation.

DuBois's ideas were also criticized as an attempt to revive an earlier organization of Booker T. Washington, the National Negro Business League (NNBL). Washington had used the League, which was founded in 1900, to promote entrepreneurial values and encourage the growth of small black businesses. Although DuBois himself had been an inspiration in the establishment of the League, it was fundamentally different from his own self-help initiative in the 1930s. The NNBL had been founded and administered according to capitalist principles. During the Great Depression DuBois, in common with other intellectuals, believed that capitalism had failed. The new black cooperatives that he advocated were to be run along socialist lines and be forerunners of the Soviet-style economies that would replace capitalism in the western world. The subtlety and complexity of DuBois's views made it difficult for him to win over popular support. This, combined with the hostility of the NAACP, prevented his proposals from ever being tried out in practice.

Nonetheless, the idea of economic self-help was taken up in a number of African American communities. In Chicago the mystic Suf Abdul Hamid organized a 'Don't Buy Where You Can't Work' campaign encouraging black customers to boycott stores that refused to hire African American workers. The same tactic was taken up by local groups in other large cities such as the New Negro Alliance of Eugene Davidson in Washington, DC.

One of the most important African American leaders of the 1930s was the socialist and trade union organizer Asa Philip Randolph. Born in Crescent City, Florida, in 1889, Randolph migrated to New York City in 1911. In 1917 he joined with fellow black socialist Chandler Owen to launch the *Messenger*, a radical African American journal. In 1925 he formed the Brotherhood of Sleeping Car Porters (BSCP), an all-black railway trade union. A prolonged struggle for employer recognition finally achieved success in 1937.

In 1935 Randolph became a co-founder and President of the National Negro Congress (NNC), created as an umbrella organization to unite black groups to confront the problems of the depression. The NNC initiated a series of 'Don't Buy Where You Can't Work' campaigns between 1935 and 1940. The NNC was unable to win the support of the NAACP, which saw it as a rival organization, and generally failed to achieve its intended goals. By 1940 it had become communist-dominated, prompting Randolph's resignation from the organization. A committed socialist, Randolph was a life-long anti-communist after the Russian Revolution of 1917.

The involvement of the Communist Party of the United States of America (CPUSA), established in 1919, was typical of the party's wider strategy in the 1930s. Unable to achieve and sustain a mass following in its own right, the party pursued a policy of co-founding ostensibly liberal and left of centre 'front' organizations which it tried to control from behind the scenes.

Communists also identified strongly with the cause of black civil rights. This was most publicly demonstrated in the Scottsboro case of 1931, when the CPUSA provided the legal defence counsel for nine black men accused of rape in Alabama. In a series of high-profile trials all the defendants were convicted. Despite strong evidence of wholesale miscarriage of justice, the last of the 'Scottsboro Nine' remained in prison until 1950.

In the 1932 presidential election the incumbent Herbert Hoover paid the penalty for America's economic woes. He was decisively defeated by the Democratic candidate Franklin Roosevelt. A liberal former Governor of the state of New York, Roosevelt had promised a 'New Deal', a reform programme to help the United States overcome the problems of the depression. On taking office, in March 1933, he introduced a far-reaching series of legislative and administrative proposals. A broad and complex range of New Deal agencies were created with the aim of achieving the three 'Rs', relief, recovery and reform. Work programmes were created to alleviate poverty and unemployment and to kick-start the American economy. The federal government assumed a more active regulatory role in an attempt to overcome structural weaknesses in the free market that had contributed to the onset of the Great Depression.

The impact of the New Deal on African Americans was mixed. A number of southern liberals were brought in to fill key positions in the Roosevelt administration. In August 1933 Clark Foreman was appointed by Roosevelt as a 'Special Adviser on the Economic Status of the Negro'. A white Georgian and former worker for the CIC, Foreman was succeeded in 1934 by his black assistant Robert Weaver. The advancement of Foreman and Weaver was testimony to the influence of Harold Ickes, Interior Secretary from 1933 to 1946. A former president of the Chicago branch of the NAACP, Ickes headed the Public Works Administration (PWA), which set up a series of large-scale spending projects to create jobs and revive the economy. The PWA spent over $45 million on the construction of black schools, hospitals and homes and provided a further $20 million in loans to states to upgrade and repair existing buildings. The PWA's Housing Division, later to become the United States Housing Authority (USHA), introduced racial quotas for its construction projects to guarantee jobs for black workers. In 1940 African Americans occupied one-third of the PWA's housing units.

Innovative liberal thinkers headed other New Deal agencies. From 1933 to 1935 Harry Hopkins, assisted by former Alabama social worker Aubrey Williams, headed the Federal Emergency Relief Administration (FERA), which spent over $4,000 million on poor relief and work projects. At local level the distribution of FERA relief was subject to racially discriminatory practices, but blacks were still major beneficiaries of the agency's expenditure. In 1935 3.5 million blacks, some 33 per cent of all African Americans, were in receipt of FERA aid. Wound up in 1935, the FERA was survived by the Works Progress Administration (WPA) which from 1936 to 1940 provided work for 350,000 African Americans each year, mainly in construction projects. WPA educational programmes employed in excess of 5,000 black teachers and taught over 250,000 African Americans to read and write.

The National Youth Administration (NYA), established in 1935, was headed by Aubrey Williams in his own right. He was aided by an African American, Mary McLeod Bethune, who was employed as a special adviser on racial issues. A former educator, Bethune served with the NYA until its termination in 1943 and was one of the highest-ranking African Americans in the Roosevelt administration. Under Williams and Bethune the NYA provided assistance and skilled training for 500,000 young black Americans.

The Farm Security Administration (FSA) was set up in 1937 to help displaced sharecroppers and agricultural labourers set up their own independent homesteads. Although short of funds, the FSA was headed by Will Alexander, a founder and Director of the CIC. Under his leadership blacks in the South received around 23 per cent of FSA aid.

Unfortunately, not all New Deal agencies were so racially enlightened. The small-scale FSA was able to provide help to only 10,000 of the 1.6 million white and black tenant farmers in the South. Much more significant for the region's future was the Agricultural Adjustment Administration (AAA). Set up in 1933, the AAA sought to halt falling farm prices by a policy of land retirement. Planters were given federal subsidies to cut back on the production of cotton and other crops. Reduced yields were then purchased by the AAA at guaranteed prices. The unfortunate consequences of this policy were highlighted by the Swedish sociologist Gunnar Myrdal in his influential 1944 study, *An American Dilemma*. Crop-reduction programmes resulted in planters and large farmers laying-off both black and white tenants and wage labourers. Between 1933 and 1940 some 200,000 black sharecroppers were evicted from their livings. Until 1936 federal compensation for reduced crop quotas was not paid to tenant farmers direct but given to planters to oversee its distribution. Intended to accommodate southern notions of racial paternalism, this practice opened up the way for wholesale abuse.

Often evicted sharecroppers received no monies at all. Those thus cheated had little chance of redress since at grassroots level the AAA's activities were monitored by local community committees dominated by the planter class.

The National Recovery Administration (NRA) was the leading New Deal agency for the business and manufacturing sector. Created in 1933, the NRA sought to introduce industrial codes of practice to eliminate child labour, set up minimum wage levels and establish maximum working hours. These agreements were drawn up jointly by representatives from business, workers and government. Lacking in force of law, the codes relied on the good will and voluntary cooperation of businesses for their enforcement. Firms that abided by the codes were awarded 'Blue Eagle' stickers to attach to their products, whilst government publicity campaigns stigmatized non-compliance as unpatriotic. One of the less successful New Deal initiatives, the NRA did little to improve conditions for white or black employees. The NRA codes excluded workers in agriculture and domestic service, sectors that accounted for around 75 per cent of all black employment. Workers in industries that were covered were little better off. Job classifications of black employees were routinely redefined and downgraded to avoid the set wage levels. Codes also allowed for geographical variations in pay. In the South wage levels were thus set lower than elsewhere in the nation to take account of the greater poverty of the region.

The racial fairness of New Deal initiatives often depended on the views and attitudes of leading administrators in each individual agency. Led by Ickes and Alexander respectively, the PWA and FSA had generally liberal racial policies. The AAA cotton section under conservative white southerner Cully Cobb was less enlightened. Similarly, the Civilian Conservation Corps (CCC), headed by Cobb's fellow Tennessean Robert Fechner, was also racially conservative. The CCC was set up in 1933 to provide the unemployed with temporary jobs in rural conservation projects; over 2.5 million workers passed through CCC camps before the agency was wound up in 1942. Although this included some 200,000 African Americans, blacks were often restricted to low-skilled jobs and camps were usually segregated.

At grassroots level deference to local custom and practice undermined the racial liberalism of New Deal projects. The Tennessee Valley Authority (TVA), set up in 1933, was one of the most radical initiatives. Covering the states of Mississippi, Alabama, Kentucky and Tennessee, the scheme sought to provide cheap hydro-electric power and create new long-term job opportunities in one of the most depressed areas of the country. At the same time the TVA was highly sensitive to the views of southern whites. Black TVA workers were given segregated facilities and accommodation and restricted to the most unskilled jobs. Similarly, even the liberal FSA and FERA tolerated discriminatory practices in their southern ventures.

Despite the inconsistencies that prevailed within and between individual government agencies, the New Deal as a whole was beneficial to African Americans. New Deal reforms were, as Gunnar Myrdal's study acknowledged, racially inclusive, even if inclusion did not always mean equality. In the 1932 presidential election over two-thirds of African American voters had supported the Republican Herbert Hoover as the heir to the party of Lincoln. In 1936, and again in 1940 and 1944, a clear majority of black voters backed the re-election of Franklin Roosevelt.

Although cautious in his public pronouncements on race relations, to avoid giving offence to influential southern Democrats in Congress, Roosevelt was still the first incumbent President since the 1870s publicly, and unequivocally, to condemn lynch mobs. Lynchings all but ceased during his presidency.

Roosevelt's appointment policy suggested a sympathy for black civil rights. In addition to white liberals like Ickes, Foreman and Alexander, over 100 African Americans served in professional and middle-ranking posts in New Deal agencies. They were collectively dubbed the 'Black Cabinet'; their appointment saw a tripling of the number of black professionals employed in the federal government bureaucracy during the 1930s.

Eleanor Roosevelt, the president's wife, was an outspoken supporter of black civil rights within the administration. She regularly attended black functions and visited New Deal projects that targeted African Americans. In 1938 she was present at the founding session of the Southern Conference for Human Welfare (SCHW) in Birmingham, Alabama. A biracial organization led mainly by southern white liberals, the SCHW sought to provide a more dynamic alternative to the CIC. In a symbolic act of defiance that received wide press coverage, Eleanor Roosevelt refused to abandon inte-grated seating arrangements when the Birmingham city authorities tried to enforce local segregation laws at the meeting.

31

In the long term, the New Deal had a number of important consequences for the development of US race relations. The scale of federal government intervention in society undermined traditional ideas of state rights. A precedent was set that made the later intervention of federal authorities in defence of black civil rights in the South in the 1950s and 1960s more likely.

Within the US legal system broad New Deal measures, and the extent of the economic crisis of the 1930s, led to changes in judicial thinking about the role of government and the courts in society. New ideas by legal thinkers like Karl Llewellyn were taught in American colleges and law schools. The American Legal Realism movement, as it came to be known, emphasized the duty of judges to consider the future social consequences of their rulings rather than just relying on past precedent.

From 1935 onwards a new generation of black lawyers rose to prominence within the NAACP. Led by Howard University Law Professor Charles Hamilton Houston and his protégé Thurgood Marshall, the NAACP's legal wing started a sustained campaign to undermine and reverse the Supreme Court's 'separate but equal' ruling in the 1896 *Plessy* case. In 1938 the case of *Missouri ex rel. Gaines* v. *Canada* was the first sign that Houston's efforts and changing legal thought were starting to have effect. The Supreme Court held that the state of Missouri was acting unconstitutionally by simply paying the tuition fees of a black student to attend a law school outside the state. The state was ordered either to build a law school for black students in Missouri or to desegregate the state's existing all-white law school. Although the 'separate but equal' ruling was also reaffirmed, the decision was the first of several Supreme Court cases that began to call into doubt the continued practical and economic viability of racial segregation.

In 1939 the NAACP and the NAACP Legal Defense and Educational Fund Inc. were split into two separate organizations. This change was made primarily for tax reasons, as the NAACP's continued lobbying for federal anti-lynching legislation meant that it was not eligible for tax-exempt status. At the same time the division reflected the growing independence and importance of the Legal Defense Fund.

Supported by a sympathetic Roosevelt administration, organized labour enjoyed a major expansion in the mid-1930s. Most notably, the 1937 Wagner Act secured the legal right of trade unions to engage in free collective bargaining. In 1935 the Congress of Industrial Organizations (CIO), an umbrella trade union body for mainly blue-collar and unskilled workers, was formed as a more radical alternative to the more traditional American Federation of Labor (AFL) set up in the 1890s. CIO activists made strong efforts to recruit black members and to work with civil rights groups.

Union organization raised the political consciousness of black workers. Young blacks educated and employed in New Deal projects also gained in hope and confidence. Helping to overcome fear and apathy, these developments constituted an important pre-condition for successful grassroots civil rights campaigns. Recent studies have suggested a clear correlation between centres of civil rights protests in the 1950s and 1960s and areas of trade union and New Deal activity. One sign of new local community awareness was the growth in both size and number of NAACP branches North and South from the late 1930s onwards. National membership of the NAACP rose from 50,000 in 1940 to almost 500,000 by 1944. Local NAACP organizers became more dynamic and less deferential to the NAACP's conservative national leadership.

The Second World War, 1939–45, had important consequences for African Americans. Increased industrial production, particularly after the entry of the United States into the war in December 1941, created new job opportunities. Between 1941 and 1946 over one million blacks left the South for employment in the North and defence industries located in the San Francisco bay area of California.

If this shift in population mirrored the Great Migration of the First World War, the attitude of black Americans to the war in 1941 to 1945 was notably different. In 1917 most blacks were either apathetic or supported US entry into the First World War. A few black spokespersons, like socialists Asa Philip Randolph and Chandler Owen, opposed the conflict, but the majority of national black leaders patriotically backed the war effort. In a famous *Crisis* editorial DuBois urged blacks to forget their grievances and 'Close Ranks' in support of the war.

During the Second World War there were signs of greater black militancy. In part this was another sign of growing political consciousness. It also reflected the sense of disillusion that many blacks had suffered at the end of the First World War. In 1918 and 1919 rather than being rewarded for their loyalty African Americans had experienced increased segregation and widespread race riots.

33

From 1941 to 1945 heightened black assertiveness was expressed in a variety of ways. If most black newspapers backed the war effort, support was not unconditional. In a phrase coined by the *Pittsburgh Courier*, blacks were urged to fight a 'double "V"' campaign in a war against Hitler abroad and discrimination at home. Significantly, although more controversial than DuBois's 1917 call to 'Close Ranks', the 'Double "V"' slogan may have been the product of conservative black opinion makers during the Second World War. The historian Lee Finkle has argued that black newspaper editors, aware of the militancy of their readers, sought to use the phrase to unite blacks in support of the war.

Capitalizing on the grassroots mood among African Americans, in January 1941 Asa Philip Randolph launched the March on Washington Movement (MOWM). Protesting at discrimination against black workers in the defence industries, Randolph threatened Roosevelt with a mass rally of 100,000 demonstrators in Washington, DC. The march was avoided when, on 25 June 1941, the President issued Executive Order number 8802 establishing a Fair Employment Practices Committee (FEPC) to monitor hiring procedures. The FEPC had limited authority and resources to counter discrimination and was wound up at the end of the war. Despite this, its existence represented an early sign of the political power of organized mass black protest.

An example of how small beginnings could lead to greater things was provided by the formation of the Congress of Racial Equality (CORE) by black and white students at the University of Chicago in June 1942. The new group was a local offshoot of the pacifist organization the Fellowship of Reconciliation (FOR); its members committed themselves to the use of non-violent direct action to oppose segregation and discrimination. Little known during the war years, CORE would become one of the five leading civil rights organizations of the 1950s and 1960s.

In the South another new, albeit ultimately less significant, organization emerged with the formation of the Southern Regional Council (SRC) in February 1944. A successor to the CIC, the SRC was also dominated by white liberals and adopted a similar gradualist philosophy. It set up interracial committees across the South to promote better race relations and sponsored research studies to provide factual information for civil rights groups.

Elsewhere in 1944 Adam Clayton Powell was elected as New York

City's first African American congressman in Harlem. During the 1950s and 1960s Powell was the nation's leading elected black politician, becoming chair of the influential House Committee on Education and Labor in 1961. A flamboyant and controversial figure, between 1961 and 1966 Powell helped to secure the passage of around 60 pieces of social reform legislation that benefited poor whites and blacks alike.

The overall impact of the Second World War was to advance further the changes set in motion during the New Deal. From 1941 to 1945 over 1 million African Americans served in the US armed forces. This experience contributed to the process of growing black grassroots consciousness. By May 1944 132,000 black US servicemen were stationed in the United Kingdom in the build-up to the D-Day invasion of 6 June. In comparison to the American South, race relations in mainland Britain were open and liberal. Black soldiers returning to the United States after the war had heightened expectations and were unwilling to accept the reimposition of old oppressions.

At home, the NAACP's legal campaign achieved an important victory in *Smith* v. *Allwright* (1944). In a case from Texas that concerned political rights, the Supreme Court held that it was unconstitutional for black voters to be excluded from Democratic Party primary elections. Despite legal obstruction and considerable violence and intimidation, black voter registration rose significantly in several southern states after the 'White Primary' ruling.

In a wider context, the extremes of Nazi racism and awareness of the Holocaust discredited scientific racism and perhaps made some white Americans feel less at ease with continued racial discrimination and segregation within the United States itself after 1945.

In contrast to the important changes taking place in US society during the 1930s and the 1940s, there were few racial advances in popular culture. Naturally, this did not preclude an occasional positive highlight. Victories by the black athlete Jesse Owens at the Berlin Olympics in 1936 made a mockery of Nazi theories of Aryan racial superiority. In 1938 African Americans across the United States shared in the triumph of Joe Louis over the German Max Schmeling to regain the title of World Heavyweight Boxing Champion. When, in 1939, the Daughters of the American Revolution (DAR) refused to allow the use of its Constitution hall for a concert by the black singer Marion Anderson, Eleanor Roosevelt typically resigned her membership in the organization. An alternative and memorable open-air performance was given by Anderson at the Lincoln memorial in Washington, DC.

The majority of black musicians and singers had less happy experiences in the 1930s. The depression marked the effective end of the Harlem Renaissance. It became harder for black artists to find white patronage or earn a living by their performances. Even Classic Blues performers like Ma Rainey (1886–1939) and Bessie Smith (1898–1937) found it hard to make a living.

In film, black moviemaker Oscar Micheaux defied all odds to turn out a series of low-budget productions for African American audiences. In mainstream Hollywood films of the 1930s stereotyped portrayals of blacks were only marginally less offensive than in the racist 1915 epic *Birth of a Nation*. Jungle films like *Tarzan the Ape-Man* (1932) and *King Kong* (1933) sought to demonstrate white supremacy in Africa as well as the United States. In *Gone with the Wind* (1939) the self-styled 'greatest film of all time' showed blacks as comic household retainers who had been happy and contented in their former slave condition. Between 1941 and 1945 productions such as *Casablanca* (1942), *Bataan* (1943) and *Lifeboat* (1944) made modest efforts to depict blacks more sympathetically in an attempt to promote racial unity for the war effort. Nonetheless, African Americans were still almost always confined to minor roles playing domestic servants and social inferiors.

In radio, the situation was no better. In the 1930s the *Amos 'n' Andy* show was easily the most popular production featuring African American characters. The lead parts in the show, which was first performed in 1926, were actually played by two whites, Freeman Gosden and Charles Correll. Assuming the roles of two comic 'darky' characters, they entertained audiences nationwide with caricatures of African American life. The modern technology of the 1930s reproduced the racist stereotypes of travelling minstrel shows first staged in the 1830s.

# CHAPTER THREE

# Montgomery spring

## Postwar change and the emergence of the civil rights movement, 1945–65

Since the 1980s there has been a growing recognition by historians of the importance of grassroots civil rights activity in the 1930s and 1940s. This has led to the rediscovery of a number of early pioneers who provided the groundwork for the later successes of the civil rights movement, 1955–68. In Virginia the black educator, journalist and minister Gordon Blaine Hancock was a campaigner against 'Jim Crowism' in his writings and lectures for approaching thirty years from the 1930s to the 1950s. He also helped found the SRC in 1944.

In Montgomery, Alabama, Vernon Johns was minister of the Dexter Avenue Baptist Church from 1948 to 1952. Several years before the Montgomery bus boycott of 1955–6 Johns courageously spoke out against racial injustice in his Sunday sermons and refused to ride the segregated city buses. Johns's radical reputation contributed to his removal from the Dexter pulpit in 1952. Ironically, the anxious church deacons in part selected his successor, Martin Luther King Jr, because he was seen as a more cautious and conservative figure.

In the neighbouring state of Louisiana Alexander Tureaud was a mainstay of the NAACP for the best part of 50 years, from 1922 to 1972. Tureaud, a lawyer, followed the NAACP's legal strategy of challenging discrimination and segregation in the courts. However, typical of the more dynamic nature of some local NAACP branches, Tureaud saw litigation not just as an end in itself but also as a means of encouraging grassroots activism.

Nationally, the civil rights policies of the Truman administration, 1945–53, reflected rising black expectations and heightened white uncertainties over the moral basis for segregation and discrimination. A southerner, from Independence, Missouri, Harry S. Truman acceded to the presidency on the death of Roosevelt in April 1945, and was re-elected in 1948. Truman's views on civil rights were shaped both by his own sense of fairness and decency and also by the less altruistic imperatives of electoral politics.

By the mid-1940s the national Democratic Party was increasingly divided on racial issues. The northern wing of the party, sensitive to the voting power of growing inner-city black populations, argued for a more liberal stance on civil rights questions. In contrast, conservative southern Democrats, who held many key positions in the party's national organization and in Congress, were strongly opposed to any changes in the status quo. These tensions came to the fore in the 1948 presidential election, a campaign in which black civil rights featured in an unusually prominent role.

This high profile dated back to a meeting between Truman and the National Emergency Committee against Mob Violence in September 1946. The committee delegation, which included Walter White, urged the President to act on widespread reports of violent racial abuse of blacks in the South. Disturbingly, there was reliable evidence that southern police forces tacitly condoned racial violence and were often active participants in such incidents. Responding to the urgings of the delegation, Truman authorized the creation of a civil rights committee to investigate the state of race relations in America. This committee, comprising respected community leaders from all walks of life – churchmen, academics, businessmen and trade unionists – sat from December 1946 to October 1947, when its final report, *To Secure These Rights*, was published.

The findings of the committee were frank and far-reaching. Highlighting the many injustices suffered by African Americans, the report put forward over 35 proposals for action. Some demands were predictable, such as the call for a federal anti-lynching law, an expansion of the civil rights section of the Justice Department and the establishment of a permanent Fair Employment Practices Commission. Other recommendations attacked the whole concept of 'Jim Crowism', calling for an end to segregation on interstate transport, the abolition of segregated public schooling in the District of Columbia, and an end to discrimination and segregation in the armed forces.

Although they were radical in tone, there was in reality little like-lihood of the committee's main proposals winning the congressional approval needed for their implementation. Nonetheless, the report attracted major national publicity and widespread condemnation from southern newspapers and congressmen. During the presidential election year of 1948 the focus on civil rights was maintained as a result of internal divisions within the Democratic Party. The Truman re-election campaign was already doomed according to the findings of opinion pollsters, which showed the president lagging well behind the Republican challenger Thomas Dewey. Truman's chances suffered a further blow with the announcement of the third-party candidacy of Henry Wallace. A former Vice-President under Franklin Roosevelt, Wallace chose to stand as the candidate of the Progressive Party. A left-wing New Dealer, Wallace was known for his commitment to black civil rights and threatened to attract the support of white liberals and African American voters who were crucial to Truman's own election prospects.

In a damage-limitation exercise Truman's campaign manager, Clark Clifford, made an important election issue of black civil rights. Truman included a strong civil rights plank in his campaign platform and became the first incumbent President to hold an election rally in Harlem. In August 1948 Truman issued Executive Order number 9981 ordering an end to segregation in the military. In his capacity as Commander in Chief of the armed forces Truman was able to implement this proposal from the *To Secure These Rights* report without having to seek congressional approval.

A high-risk strategy to limit the defection of liberal supporters, Truman's civil rights initiatives inevitably infuriated conservative southern Democrats. At the Democratic Party National Convention in 1948 Strom Thurmond of South Carolina led a walkout of disaffected delegates. Bringing about a second split within the party, Thurmond himself stood as an independent state rights candidate in the election.

In the event, the Democratic Party's divisions notwithstanding, Truman narrowly secured re-election in November 1948, defeating Dewey by a margin of just over 2 million votes. Despite the fact that 66 per cent of African Americans had supported him there were no major initiatives on civil rights during Truman's second administration, 1949–53. In part this reflected the extent to which the President's earlier civil rights agenda had been shaped by tempo-rary electoral needs as opposed to genuine long-term commitment. The onset of the Korean War, 1950–3, further distracted attention from civil rights issues.

In domestic politics the blossoming of civil rights campaigns that had seemed likely at the end of the Second World War was blighted by the new climate of Cold War politics. The onset of the Cold War by 1947 not only had major international ramifications but also had a profound impact on the United States. Growing anti-communism led to the distrust and persecution of trade unionists and liberal thinkers, who came to be perceived as subversives. In 1949 15 states passed anti-subversion laws and nearly 1 million left-wing members were expelled from the CIO. Official and public hysteria reached a peak in the years 1950–4, the era of 'McCarthyism'.

In a speech at Wheeling, Virginia, on 9 February 1950, US Senator Joseph McCarthy claimed knowledge of widespread communist infiltration in the federal government. Although lacking in supportive evidence, McCarthy's often repeated and exaggerated assertions raised the persecution of radicals and left-wing causes to the level of a witch-hunt. The congressional House Un-American Activities Committee interrogated hundreds of suspected communist sympa-thizers. In 1951 the state of Tennessee introduced the death penalty for anyone who merely advocated communist ideas. The normally liberal New England state of Massachusetts introduced a three-year prison sentence for anyone convicted of allowing a Communist Party meeting to be held in their own home.

Historians have differed in their assessment of the relationship between anti-communism and black civil rights. In some respects Cold War tensions were a positive force. Between 1947 and 1969 successive US Presidents, Truman, Eisenhower, Kennedy and Johnson, expressed concern at the negative international publicity that the United States received as a result of the treatment of its own black citizens. Soviet propaganda exploited this source of embarrassment to the full. During a two-week period in May 1963, the culmination of the major civil rights campaign in Birmingham, Alabama, prompted over 1,400 anti-American commentaries world-wide by Soviet writers and broadcasters.

Media offensives of this sort were all the more damaging by the late 1950s as the United States and the Soviet Union competed to win the allegiance of newly independent black African nations and other developing countries. The increasing pace of Third World de-colonization was also felt within the United States. Growing numbers of black African students enrolled in American colleges and universities. Diplomats from newly de-colonized nations took up posts as embassy staff in Washington, DC and as part of national delegations at the headquarters of the United Nations (UN), established in New York City in 1945.

Newcomers from the Third World acted as sources of encouragement to African Americans in the pursuit of civil rights. There was also the ever-present possibility of some international incident if black African diplomatic personnel were subjected to 'Jim Crow' treatment in the South. In an incident in 1961 the ambassador for Chad complained to newly elected President John F. Kennedy that he had been forcibly ejected from a restaurant in Maryland. Kennedy, himself a former chair of the US Senate Subcommittee on Africa, used the State Department to secure a public apology from the Governor of Maryland.

In the immediate postwar years civil rights leaders in America sought to use the UN as an international forum to embarrass the federal government over the treatment of its black population. On 6 June 1946, the NNC presented the UN with 'A Petition on Behalf of Thirteen Million Oppressed Negro Citizens of the United States of America'. Even the more conservative NAACP put forward 'An Appeal to the World: A Statement of the Denial of Human Rights of Minorities in the Case of Citizens of Negro Descent in the United States of America, and an Appeal to the United Nations for Redress'.

By the end of the 1940s, however, the prevailing mood of anti-communism made such initiatives all but impossible. Public criticism of race relations in the United States was increasingly seen as unpatriotic and the product of Soviet agitation. In 1949 the left-wing African American singer and actor Paul Robeson praised the Soviet Union and denounced US policy towards Africa as 'similar to that of Hitler and Goebbels'. Retaliation was swift. Robeson found it impossible to find employment and his career was effectively ruined for several years. In 1950 his passport was revoked, which cut off the possibility of work overseas.

In February 1951 the veteran civil rights campaigner W. E. B. DuBois was arrested as a suspected Soviet agent. Although all charges against him were dropped by November, for lack of evidence, DuBois also had his passport revoked. In acts of Orwellian repression, his many books and articles were systematically removed from college and public libraries for several years. Less-known black radicals fared even worse, being subject to loss of employment and even imprisonment.

Mainstream civil rights groups and leaders, like Walter White and the NAACP, often sided with the forces of repression in the McCarthy years. In 1948 the Executive Committee and Annual Convention of CORE passed anti-communist resolutions repudiating all links with communist-infiltrated organizations. Individual CORE branches, or chapters, were ordered to cease contact with communists or themselves face expulsion. In 1950 the NAACP launched its own internal investigation of suspected communist sympathizers and the NAACP Board of Directors were authorized to expel individual members or even whole branches. In 1952 Asa Philip Randolph embarked on a speaking tour of Asia, with the white socialist leader Norman Thomas, and denounced communism whilst praising recent progress in race relations within the United States. In the case of Randolph, a longstanding anti-communist, this was as much motivated by genuine conviction as it was an exercise in national flag waving.

In one sense the anti-communist purges of the late 1940s and early 1950s helped civil rights groups to regain self-autonomy, reversing the communist entry-ism of the 1930s. In demonstrating their loyalty and patriotism civil rights leaders also hoped to earn the sympathy of politicians and to avoid civil rights being labelled a subversive issue. In the event this expectation proved over-optimistic. Southern national and state leaders were all too successful in using anti-communism as a justification for the official persecution and oppression of civil rights groups. Efforts by civil rights organizations to demonstrate their patriotism by the expulsion of suspected communists only seemed to substantiate the original charge that civil rights was a communist propaganda issue. Despite its 1948 'Statement on Communism', CORE went into a period of sharp decline between 1950 and 1954, in terms of both membership and finances as contributions from outside donors collapsed.

The NAACP fared equally badly. Within the South individual NAACP members were targeted for both physical and economic persecution. Southern state legislatures denounced the organization as communistic and passed legislation that required NAACP branches to publish membership lists. Ironically, the state legislature of Louisiana evoked its 1924 Fuqua Act, originally passed as an anti-Ku Klux Klan measure, to force public disclosure of the names of NAACP members. When NAACP chapters refused to comply with such demands, southern state courts responded with injunctions prohibiting all NAACP activity. By 1957 the NAACP was outlawed in Alabama and fighting lawsuits to maintain its survival in eight other southern states.

Even moderate white organizations known for their civil rights sympathies did not escape persecution. In June 1947 the SCHW was denounced as a communist front by the congressional House Un-American Activities Committee (HUAC). Unable to recover from this tarnishing of its image, the SCHW ceased existence in 1949, leaving behind only its tax-exempt offshoot, the Southern Conference Educational Fund (SCEF). In March 1954 even the SCEF became the subject of public loyalty hearings before the US Senate Internal Security Subcommittee, enthusiastically chaired by arch segregationist James Eastland of Mississippi.

Taken as a whole, although the anti-communism of the late Truman and early Eisenhower years brought some limited pluses to the cause of black civil rights, these were more than offset by the minuses. The domestic impact of the Cold War, more than any other single factor, helps to explain why the civil rights movement in its most widely recognized form did not emerge until the mid-1950s rather than in the late 1940s.

Nationally, the worst excesses of McCarthyism subsided after 1954. McCarthy himself was publicly discredited and died as a result of alcoholism in 1957. In the South, however, anti-communism remained a potent force for several more years. Largely the result of cynical manipulation, this persistence also in part reflected the feeling of white southerners that the civil rights movement embodied a centralizing Soviet-style philosophy that was directed against the freedoms of individual whites and southern regional identity. Well into the 1960s Martin Luther King was regularly denounced by southern whites as a communist sympathizer, allegations that were given added credence by the support they received from J. Edgar Hoover, National Director of the Federal Bureau of Investigation (FBI).

Although organizations like the NAACP and CORE did ultimately survive the excesses of McCarthyism, they were fundamentally changed by the experience. Most importantly, links between civil rights protest and organized labour, which had developed during the New Deal, withered away. In their respective spheres both civil rights organizations and labour unions were forced to cut back on their wider social programmes and associations in order to concentrate on more inward-looking strategies directed at self-preservation and survival. In consequence, civil right groups during the 1950s and early 1960s focused largely on issues like voting rights and desegregation, neglecting other basic concerns like poverty and economic inequality. When attention was finally directed to these areas, in the mid-1960s, the response of the mainstream civil rights organizations was often too little, too late. The inadequacy of this reaction acted as a catalyst for the break-up of the civil rights movement in the years 1965–8 and the emergence of the philosophy of 'Black Power'.

In legal, as well as political, terms the year 1954 was a watershed for black civil rights. This was because of the far-reaching decision of the US Supreme Court in the case of *Brown* v. *The Topeka Board of Education*. Collectively contesting a series of earlier school segregation rulings that had been given by lower courts, the *Brown* case was brought before the Supreme Court in 1953 by Thurgood Marshall of the NAACP Legal Defense Fund. In May 1954 the court, led by its new Chief Justice, Earl Warren, held in a unanimous decision that school segregation was unconstitutional. This marked a direct reversal of the *Plessy* 'separate but equal' ruling of 1896. The court did not seek to rebut systematically the rationale of *Plessy* but rather relied on a set of seven social science studies. These suggested that irrespective of the quality of education given to black and white pupils, the existence of segregated schools created an innate feeling of inferiority in the minds of black children. Separate was therefore by its very nature unequal, and as such unconstitutional.

Responding to the perceived need for change, the decision of the Warren Court reflected developments in US legal thinking that had been taking place since the 1930s with the emergence of the American Legal Realism movement. By the 1950s American Legal Realism was the dominant philosophy in US law schools. Despite this, the thinking of the Warren Court in *Brown* was regarded as controversial, even by some supporters of desegregation. It was undeniable that the quality of education provided for most black children in the South was grossly inferior to that available to white pupils. The logic of the court's judgement, however, was that what mattered was not so much the actual nature of the provision as the perception that black children had of it. If commendable in providing a justification for desegregation, this line of thought set an uncomfortable precedent in legal terms.

The practical consequences of the *Brown* decision, like the philosophy behind it, have been a subject of much debate. *Brown*, as observed by historian Mary Ellison, has often been billed as 'the avenging angel of a gothic tragedy'. On this interpretation, decades of injustice were cast aside in one moment. Moreover, African Americans were given renewed hope of achieving ultimate equality within American society, which encouraged the mass protests of the civil rights movement, 1955–68. Although there is some truth in this perception, there had been a gradual, steady increase in grassroots civil rights protest for some time, as has already been noted. A powerful civil rights momentum was established well before *Brown*.

Similarly, in a legal sense, the *Brown* judgement was not so much lightning from a clear sky as the culmination of a series of Supreme Court decisions dating back to the 1930s. These had introduced increasingly stringent standards that states had to meet if they wished to practise segregation. In the case of *Sweatt v. Painter* (1950), a 3 million dollar upgrading of the black Prairie View University in Texas was thus ruled insufficient to meet the criteria of 'separate but equal'. The Supreme Court reasoned that bricks and mortar were not the only yardsticks of equality: less tangible factors like tradition and academic prestige also mattered.

The *Sweatt* case and other Supreme Court rulings had clearly raised the possibility that a rejection of the whole principle of segregation was only a matter of time. Despite this, the reaction of whites in the South to the *Brown* decision was one of surprise and outrage. In a prelude to the so-called 'Massive Resistance' of southern whites to desegregation, White Citizens' Councils were set up in almost all southern cities. The Councils, dubbed a 'country club Klan' by southern white journalist Hodding Carter, were the more influential because they were composed mainly of middle- to upper-income whites from business and the professions. On the political front the 'Southern Manifesto' of March 1956, drafted by US Senator Sam Ervin Jr of North Carolina, pledged to maintain segregation by all legal means and was signed by over 100 congressmen from the former Confederate states.

On 31 May 1955 the Supreme Court, responding to both southern reactions and the administrative problems of school desegregation, issued a follow-up ruling to *Brown*. The court recognized that the full integration of schools could not be achieved immediately, because of practical difficulties in respect of the provision of school buildings and teaching staff. Consequently, southern school boards were instructed to implement *Brown* 'with all deliberate speed', but without any fixed timetable laid down for the completion of desegregation. Rather than encourage compliance with the law the guidelines only strengthened opposition to it. School boards throughout the South, where they were prepared to recognize the legitimacy of *Brown* at all, drew up convoluted desegregation plans that would have required decades to achieve full integration.

In the face of this procrastination some liberal commentators who had praised the initial *Brown* decision were highly critical of the court for the 'with all deliberate speed' caveat. 'Justice too long delayed' was effectively 'justice denied'. To overcome southern delaying tactics the NAACP and other civil rights groups would have had to take all of the hundreds of school boards throughout the South to court on an individual basis to challenge their desegregation plans. This would have been a nigh-on impossible task; matters were made more difficult by the refusal of President Eisenhower, 1953–61, to endorse the *Brown* ruling publicly. He cited constitutional propriety to justify his silence, that it would be improper for an incumbent President to comment on a Supreme Court ruling. His inaction was widely interpreted in the South as a sign of his opposition to enforced school desegregation.

To complicate matters further, in many districts of the South, as well as the urban North, separate schooling for whites and blacks persisted for geographical and locational reasons – *de facto* segregation – as well as because of a deliberate refusal to integrate. To put it simply, white suburban residents sent their children to virtually all-white schools situated on the edge of city boundaries. Conversely, black ghetto pupils attended effectively all-black inner-city schools.

All these factors combined meant that despite the bold rhetoric of the Warren Court in its original *Brown* ruling, in practice widespread school segregation enforced by state and local authorities continued in the South until the late 1960s and early 1970s. The more intractable problem of *de facto* school segregation persisted even longer.

The policies and attitudes of US presidential administrations in the 1950s and 1960s were arguably of greater significance to the struggle for black civil rights than the actions of the Supreme Court. Since the 1980s the judgement of historians on the overall performance of the Republican Eisenhower administrations, 1953–61, has tended to be favourable. Eisenhower's ability to maintain economic prosperity at home, and peace and stability during difficult times in international affairs, has been increasingly recognized and praised. His record on black civil rights, where change rather than continuity was required, was less successful.

Conservative by nature, Eisenhower, a soldier turned statesman, had spent most of his adult life in the armed forces. Career postings at military bases in the South, and many southern white friends, meant that he was both intellectually and temperamentally unsuited to recognizing the need for reform in race relations. In 1948 he had strongly opposed Truman's desegregation of the armed forces. When he was President in his own right Eisenhower's views suggested little capacity for change. Although there was a steady move towards the desegregation of public facilities in Washington, DC during the Eisenhower years, this was more the result of action by Congress than the President.

Eisenhower's response to the *Brown* case was typical of his approach. Prior to the court's ruling Eisenhower encouraged Chief Justice Earl Warren to reaffirm the 'separate but equal' doctrine. When the court's decision was announced the President's public display of neutrality was undermined by evidence of his private disapproval. In his memoirs, published after leaving office, Eisenhower later admitted that he had not agreed with 'those who had believed that legislation alone could instigate instant morality, or who believed that coercion could cure all civil rights problems'. The difficulty with this cautious approach was that a philosophy of gradualism all too easily translated into a practical policy of doing nothing at all.

During his second administration, 1957–61, Eisenhower did show some signs of greater decisiveness. In September 1957 he sent over 1,000 US paratroopers to the Little Rock High School in Arkansas to enforce the admission of nine black children. The need to back *Brown* publicly was, however, only one of several factors that led Eisenhower to act. There was an urgent need to maintain public order and avoid bloodshed after angry segregationist mobs had surrounded the school to prevent the entry of the black pupils. Presidential dignity and authority were also at stake after the Governor of Arkansas, Orval Faubus, had appeared to renege on a private agreement with Eisenhower to resolve the crisis.

Eisenhower's last years in office saw the passage of the 1957 and 1960 Civil Rights Acts, the first civil rights legislation passed by Congress since the Reconstruction era. The aim of the two Acts was to provide federal judges with greater supervisory jurisdiction over the registration of black voters in the South. In the event both bills were badly compromised, at the hands of southern conservatives in Congress, and lacked any real coercive authority. Even mainstream civil rights leaders like Martin Luther King and Roy Wilkins, Executive Secretary of the NAACP since 1955, were unwilling to give enthusiastic support to the new measures.

Eisenhower's preferred response to racial issues was to avoid involvement or action whenever possible. In 1955 he refused to speak out publicly after the lynching of Emmett Till, a 14-year-old African American, in Mississippi. Throughout his years in office Eisenhower sought to avoid meeting with black civil rights leaders. The appointment of Frederic Morrow, an African American, as Personal Administrative Assistant to the President was more symbolic than significant. Morrow's responsibilities were largely clerical, involving little input into actual policy making. Prime responsibility for civil rights was delegated by Eisenhower to Vice-President Richard Nixon and to Maxwell Rabb, a white advisor on minority interests.

In November 1960, the election to the presidency of the more dynamic and youthful 43-year-old Democrat John F. Kennedy marked an apparent departure from the inertia of the Eisenhower years. In the election campaign Kennedy made a strong personal commitment on civil rights, promising, if elected, to end discrimination in federal housing projects 'at the stroke of a pen'. In October 1960, less than one month before election-day, Martin Luther King was sentenced to four months' imprisonment for participation in a sit-in protest in Atlanta. In contrast to the cautious inaction of the Republican candidate, Richard Nixon, Kennedy responded with a personal telephone call to King's wife, Coretta Scott, to assure her of his support. Combining action with words, the candidate's brother, Robert Kennedy, used his influence to persuade the Georgia state judge in the case to authorize King's release from jail the following day. Appreciation of this action by African Americans was a key factor in the outcome of the election. In November Kennedy narrowly defeated Nixon by a margin of under 110,000 in the popular vote in one of the most tightly contested presidential elections in US history. Seventy-five per cent of African American voters had supported Kennedy.

The civil rights record of the Kennedy administration, 1961–3, was mixed. On taking office the new President appointed over 40 African Americans to important positions in government. Thurgood Marshall, the NAACP's lead lawyer in the *Brown* case, was made Solicitor General. Robert Weaver became head of the Housing and Home Finance Agency. George Weaver was made Assistant Secretary of Labor and Lisle Carter Assistant Secretary at the Department of Health, Education and Welfare. Carl Rowan was appointed first as Assistant Secretary of State and then as Ambassador to Finland. A white lawyer, Harris Wofford, was appointed as Special Assistant to the President on civil rights.

Other appointments were less enlightened. Appeasing the Dixiecrat wing of his party, Kennedy nominated a number of racial conservatives to southern district courts and the federal fifth circuit. One nominee, Harold Cox, had even been known to refer to blacks as 'chimpanzees' in his directions from the bench.

The federal fifth circuit, which covered Georgia, Florida, Alabama, Mississippi, Louisiana and Texas, was of particular significance. Judges appointed to this circuit had the responsibility of ensuring that desegregation decisions of higher courts were enforced at local level. Eisenhower's appointees to the fifth circuit had generally been supportive of integration, but some 25 to 33 per cent of Kennedy nominees had a pro-segregationist background or reputation.

In terms of moral leadership of the nation Kennedy's record was positive. He frequently met with civil rights spokespersons. African Americans were regularly invited to receptions at the White House, and the President resigned from the prestigious Cosmos Club because of its refusal to admit blacks as members. This marked a refreshing change from Eisenhower, who had not even felt comfortable in the presence of African Americans.

Less encouragingly, exemplary personal conduct sometimes became a substitute for direct executive action. In January 1963 Martin Luther King urged the President to mark the one hundredth anniversary of the Emancipation Proclamation by issuing a second emancipation proclamation against segregation. Rejecting such a measure as too radical, Kennedy instead commemorated the occasion with a social gathering for leading African Americans at the White House.

In April 1961 presidential Executive Order number 10925 provided better employment opportunities for blacks in the federal government. Executive Order number 11063 fulfilled the campaign pledge to end segregation in federal housing, but this came only on 20 November 1962, after the mid-term congressional elections, rather than 'at the stroke of a pen'. The order was also narrow in scope, applying only to new federal construction projects rather than pre-existing housing.

In his dealings with Congress, Kennedy secured the passage of no civil rights legislation, though on 11 June 1963, five months before his assassination, he did announce a proposed civil rights bill. If this was late in the day such tardiness was understandable. The narrowness of Kennedy's election victory in 1960 did not give a mandate for sweeping early reforms. The inevitable opposition of southern Democrats in Congress meant that the successful passage of any civil rights legislation was far from guaranteed. Moreover, domestic policy in the early days of the Kennedy administration was dominated by the President's 'New Frontier' programme. A package of reform measures aimed at extending the social and economic legislation of the New Deal, the New Frontier depended on the support of southern congressmen. These initiatives were of particular benefit to African Americans, who constituted the poorest and most disadvantaged group in US society.

Holding office at the height of the Cold War, Kennedy himself saw foreign policy and superpower relations as his main priority as President. In consequence the main responsibility for civil rights was delegated to Robert Kennedy as Attorney General. Although broadly sympathetic towards the cause of racial equality, the younger Kennedy generally responded to events rather than initiating them.

In 1961 the CORE 'Freedom Rides' marked the first major test of the Attorney General's resolve. In the case of *Boynton* v. *Virginia*, in December 1960, the Supreme Court ruled that interstate bus transportation and bus terminals should be desegregated. In May the following year, in an attempt to enforce this decision, 23 CORE volunteers boarded Trailways and Greyhound buses in Washington,

DC that were bound for the South. Between 14 and 20 May, the refusal of the freedom riders to accept segregated seating and facilities at Anniston, Birmingham and Montgomery, all in Alabama, resulted in horrifying violent attacks by local white segregationist mobs. Forced to act, Robert Kennedy negotiated with local state and city officials to secure the safe passage of the riders. In September, under pressure from the Attorney General, the federal Interstate Commerce Commission (ICC) issued an order prohibiting segregated facilities in interstate travel.

In September 1962 the admission of James Meredith as the first black student at the University of Mississippi led to another crisis. The initial response of the President and his brother was again to maintain a policy of federal non-involvement. They sought to defuse events by brokering a behind-the-scenes settlement with the Governor of Mississippi, Ross Barnett. When on 1 October segregationist mobs besieged Meredith, and federal marshals protecting him at the University, the Kennedys finally took decisive action, sending in 30,000 troops to restore order.

Assassinated in Dallas, Texas, on 22 November 1963, John F. Kennedy was succeeded as the nation's chief executive by Vice-President Lyndon Johnson. Seeing out the remainder of Kennedy's term of office, Johnson was elected President in his own right in November 1964, remaining in the White House until January 1969. Despite his Texan background Johnson supported the cause of black civil rights more vigorously than either of his immediate predecessors. During his period of office he made over 200 speeches with a significant civil rights theme, and secured the passage of three major pieces of civil rights legislation.

The Civil Rights Act of 1964 brought to fruition the bill introduced by Kennedy in 1963. An omnibus law with many provisions, the 1964 Act gave the federal government wide-ranging powers to end segregation and discrimination in employment, schooling and public facilities and accommodation. In 1965 the Voting Rights Act provided the federal authorities with strong and incisive powers to oversee the registration of black voters in the South. In another initiative the 1968 Civil Rights Act provided for more effective means to end segregation and discrimination in federal housing projects.

Although these measures reflected a genuine commitment by Johnson to greater racial equality, it should be noted that the climate for action was more favourable in these years. The enormous feeling of public sympathy for the assassinated Kennedy undermined the potential for southern opposition in Congress to the 1964 Act, which had been one of the martyred President's last major initiatives. In November 1964 Johnson's overwhelming electoral defeat of Republican presidential candidate Barry Goldwater provided a decisive mandate for action that Kennedy had never enjoyed. Similarly, the Housing Act of 6 April 1968 was passed at a time of heightened public and congressional support for civil rights following the assassination of Martin Luther King only two days before.

More than any President, Martin Luther King is the figure most closely associated with the advances made by the civil rights movement in the years 1955–65. Born in Atlanta, Georgia, in 1929, King studied at the city's prestigious black Morehouse College before enrolling at Crozer Theological Seminary in Chester, Pennsylvania in 1948 to study for the ministry. Following his graduation in 1951 he moved on to Boston University to study for a Ph.D. On completion of his doctorate, in 1954, King secured his first full ministerial appointment as pastor of Dexter Avenue Baptist Church in Montgomery, Alabama, taking up the position recently vacated by Vernon Johns.

In December 1955 the little-known King, only 26 years old and a newcomer to the city, reluctantly agreed to accept the leadership of a bus boycott campaign already initiated by the local black community. The inspiration for the campaign had come from local NAACP activist E. D. Nixon and Jo Ann Robinson of the Montgomery Women's Political Council. The involvement of the Council, founded in 1946 and inspired by Vernon Johns, reflected the central role often played by women in southern civil rights protest both before and after the Second World War.

The 1955 boycott reached a successful conclusion on 13 November 1956 when the US Supreme Court declared Alabama's state and city segregation laws relating to public transport to be unconstitutional. By this time the charismatic King had acquired the status of a national celebrity. King's mesmerizing oratorical ability, and the aura of martyrdom that has surrounded him since his assassination, makes an objective assessment of his contribution as a civil rights leader difficult, bordering on irreverent. In popular perception and mythology the personality of Martin Luther King has become so inter-linked with the struggle for racial equality that his emergence as a national spokesperson in 1955 and his death thirteen years later in 1968 are usually seen as marking the beginning and the end of the postwar civil rights movement.

The reality was more complex. Historical research on King since the 1960s has revealed evidence of his serial marital infidelities and the extensive use of plagiarism in his Ph.D. dissertation and public speeches. In addition to his great strengths he also possessed human frailties and weaknesses.

Acknowledgement of this inevitable truth quickened historiographical trends already underway. It is now recognized that civil rights campaigns were more than just an extension of the personality of Dr King. The Montgomery bus boycott would have taken place without him, for it was not he who initiated it. The major civil rights campaigns of the 1950s and 1960s were not the by-products of his messianic persona, but rather the culmination of growing black consciousness and protest at grassroots level that dated back to the 1930s and 1940s. Similarly, the break-up of the civil rights coalition was already underway before King's death and a result of complex political, social and economic factors. During his lifetime Martin Luther King's leadership was a subject of criticism even within the civil rights movement. His successful campaigns were offset by, at times, bitter disappointments, failure and self-doubt.

In January 1957, seeking to build on the success of the Montgomery campaign, King organized a 'Southern Negro Leaders' Conference on Transportation and Integration' in Atlanta. Largely attended by southern black churchmen, known to King through the network of the National Baptist Convention (NBC), the conference marked a turning point in civil rights protest. Recognition was given to the need for the interregional coordination of localized protests. There was also an acknowledgement of the important contribution church leaders and their congregations could make to civil rights protests.

In a follow-up conference in February, discussion turned to practical organization with the creation of the Southern Christian Leadership Conference (SCLC). Operating almost exclusively within the South, and with King as its president, the all-black SCLC was dominated by Baptist ministers. Contrary to popular perception the great majority of southern black churchmen did not become active participants in the civil rights struggles of the 1950s and 1960s. Nonetheless, the formation of the SCLC had a major impact in adding the moral authority of the church to civil rights campaigns. At a practical level church ministers were usually well-respected members of their local communities, and experienced in coordinating and organizing neighbourhood activities. Moreover, the SCLC filled a void in national civil rights organization in the 1950s.

At this time CORE was largely northern-based in its operations and at the nadir of its Cold War decline. The NAACP was still struggling for its very survival in the southern states. Furthermore, the conservative national leadership of the organization was committed to the NAACP's traditional legalistic approach, seeking to challenge segregation in the courts rather than through direct-action campaigns.

The SCLC as a Christian organization composed mainly of black clergymen could not easily be depicted as a communist front. Its southern centre of gravity provided civil rights leadership where it was needed most. Its focus on organizing local protest campaigns was a crucial means of following up in practice the legal victories achieved by the NAACP in the courts. In combination with the NAACP, NUL, CORE and the Student Nonviolent Coordinating Committee (SNCC), formed in 1960, the SCLC was one of the five great organizations that bound together the civil rights movement.

Despite the inevitable tensions, rivalries and disagreements between these groups, one of the greatest achievements of Martin Luther King in these years was to keep together this, often fractious, civil rights coalition. Rising above petty partisanship, King regularly gave public praise and recognition to the achievements of all civil rights groups, not just the SCLC. In financial terms he was similarly a tireless fundraiser for all, not just the one. Moreover, King's diplomacy and moral authority enabled him to appeal to the better instincts of individuals within all the major civil rights organizations, whatever their personal and ideological differences. In a wider sense, as the historian August Meier has noted, King occupied the 'vital center' of the civil rights movement. More than any other individual he was able to articulate the anger and frustration of black protesters in a way that could still retain the sympathy of northern white liberals.

Nonetheless, success was often accompanied by setback. In 1958–60 the SCLC's first major campaign, the 'Crusade for Citizenship', aimed at doubling black voter registration in the South, had only limited impact because of poor coordination and inadequate finances. The fact that the moral power of non-violent protest, to which King was so deeply committed, could not achieve victories in the absence of careful planning and organization was further demonstrated by events in Albany, Georgia, during 1961–2. Responding to requests from local organizers, in December 1961 King visited Georgia to support an SNCC-inspired campaign that was already underway in the city. Initially intended as only a brief visit King actually remained in Albany to direct protests until the following summer.

In contrast to the lack of pre-planning by the SCLC, King's effective opponent in the city, Police Chief Laurie Pritchett, had given careful thought as to the best strategy to counter the protests. In prearranged agreements protesters arrested in mass were transported to jails in surrounding townships, which alleviated the problem of a shortage of holding cells in Albany itself. Pritchett was sensitive to national and international media attention and ensured that there was a minimum use of force by police against demonstrators. He even joined King in public prayers. When King himself was arrested Pritchett quickly arranged for the court fine to be paid by an anonymous donor to secure the early release of the SCLC leader. Unable to make progress against such tactics, King left Albany in August 1962 with little having been accomplished.

Following these early failures King's greatest successes came in the years 1963–5. In April and May 1963 King led a major civil rights campaign in Birmingham, Alabama. Lessons were learnt from the mistakes of Albany: the protests were carefully prepared in advance by Wyatt Walker, the Executive Director of the SCLC, in a secret strategy document, 'Project "C" for Confrontation'. The abrasive police commissioner of Birmingham, Eugene 'Bull' Conner, lacked the guile of Pritchett and used fire-hoses and police dogs against the demonstrators, including pregnant women and school children. In the peace agreement that was reached between civil rights negotiators and local businessmen, on 10 May 1963, only limited concessions were made towards desegregation. Despite this, the shocking tactics that Conner had employed provided the civil rights movement with a significant moral victory and considerable favourable media attention, both national and worldwide.

On 28 August 1963 King's 'I Have a Dream' speech before a crowd of 250,000 supporters at the Lincoln memorial in Washington, DC constituted the high point of the March on Washington jointly sponsored by all the major civil rights organizations. On

10 December the following year King was awarded the prestigious Nobel Peace Prize in Norway.

At the height of his powers, in March 1965, King assumed the leadership of a 50-mile march by civil rights protesters from Selma to Montgomery, Alabama, in support of the Voting Rights Bill then being considered by Congress. An initial march had already ended in failure on 'Bloody Sunday', 7 March, with demonstrators beaten and tear gassed by state troopers at the Pettus bridge on the outskirts of Selma. King's initiative at first appeared to be equally unsuccessful when, again confronted by state troopers, he ordered the marchers to return towards Selma. On 17 March, however, a federal judge approved the proposed protest and President Johnson placed state troopers under federal control to protect the participants. From 21 to 25 March King finally led protesters from Selma to Montgomery in what had become a victory celebration.

Even during these years of triumph King was not immune from criticism. In 1963 the militant Black Muslim leader Malcolm X denounced King for exposing school children to police violence during the Birmingham campaign. Radicals within the civil rights movement saw the Birmingham peace agreement and the abandonment of King's first Selma march as conservative compromises and signs of weakness.

Much of the criticism directed at King came from within the ranks of the most recently founded of the leading civil rights organizations, the Student Nonviolent Coordinating Committee (SNCC). 'Snick', as it became known, had its origins in 1960. In February that year four students at North Carolina Agricultural and Technical College, Franklin McCain, David Richmond, Joseph McNeil and Izell Blair, demanded service at the whites only section of the Woolworth's cafeteria in Greensboro, North Carolina. When staff refused to take their orders they remained seated until the store's closing time. This minor incident marked the emergence of the 'sit-in' as a major form of civil rights protest. Within a week the protest had escalated to the point where hundreds of students had become involved and the Woolworth's manager was forced to close the store. In earlier years this affair may have received only local attention. In 1960 the newly developed interregional links and awareness that prevailed among civil rights groups meant that between February and April copycat sit-ins spread throughout the South, principally involving student protesters.

Looking to take full advantage of this development, Ella Baker, then acting Executive Director of the SCLC, organized a student convention at Raleigh, North Carolina from 16 to 18 April 1960. It was from this conference that the SNCC, the youth wing of the civil rights movement, emerged. The role of Baker, both within the SCLC and in the creation of the SNCC, was a further example of the important part played by women activists in civil rights organizations.

The founding of the SNCC, although ultimately of great significance, brought no dramatic early results. Chronically short of funds, the SNCC was able to achieve little in its early years. In 1961 it had only one full-time, but rarely paid, member of staff, Bob Moses, whose office comprised a small section within the SCLC headquarters in Atlanta.

During the spring of 1961, at the invitation of Amzie Moore, a veteran NAACP worker, Moses launched a voter registration campaign in McComb, a small town in south-east Mississippi. In these years the Kennedy administration was keen to encourage voter registration work as a less controversial alternative to other forms of civil rights activity. The private Taconic Foundation was prepared to provide substantial funding for voter registration projects. Faced with this incentive the SNCC increasingly channelled its membership into this work.

Initially, SNCC members were divided on this strategy. Some activists saw voter registration as a tame, conservative option in comparison to direct action protests. In fact, the opposite proved to be the case. Concentrated in Mississippi, the most reactionary of all southern states, the SNCC's voter registration work often provoked no less violent responses than boycotts, marches or sit-ins. In order to win over the confidence of long-oppressed African Americans in rural Mississippi, SNCC workers lived and worked in these communities for months, even years, at a time. This shared poverty and deprivation had the effect of radicalizing SNCC workers, many of whom came from middle-class backgrounds.

This was visibly reflected in the changing sartorial preferences of SNCC personnel. Most of the students attending the founding conference of the SNCC in 1960 had worn conservative suits or dresses. By 1963 blue denim overalls had become the unofficial uniform of SNCC activists. Grassroots community programmes also developed within the SNCC an already-present trend towards democratic decentralization. SNCC workers increasingly came to resent the hierarchical, leader-centred approach associated with Martin Luther King and the SCLC. Instead it was believed that local communities should be empowered to act and think for themselves through the development of freedom schools and other neighbourhood cultural programmes.

The SNCC's greatest achievements came in June to August 1964 with the 'Mississippi Summer Project'. Under the auspices of the Council of Federated Organizations (COFO), an umbrella organization formed to coordinate the work of civil rights groups in Mississippi, thousands of SNCC volunteers entered into the Magnolia State.

A demonstration of the growing confidence and success of the civil rights movement, the Mississippi Summer Project concealed growing inner tensions and conflicts. Impatient at the slow pace of reform under the Kennedy administration, John Lewis, the main SNCC speaker at the March on Washington in August 1963, initially threatened to disrupt the harmony of the occasion with a prepared speech that was highly critical of the President. Unity was only maintained when, minutes before mounting the podium, Lewis toned down his rhetoric at the personal request of the veteran civil rights campaigner Asa Philip Randolph.

During the summer of 1964, unable to register to vote through official state channels, SNCC workers encouraged black Mississippians to join the Mississippi Freedom Democratic Party (MFDP), which held its own shadow elections for political office. In August, MFDP members sought to claim the seats of the official Mississippi delegation at the Democratic Party National Convention in Atlantic City, New Jersey.

In a compromise settlement inspired by Lyndon Johnson, the Convention's Credentials Committee offered the MFDP two seats at large, but without official delegate status, and the prospect of interracial delegations at future conventions. In response to this all but two of the official all-white delegation from Mississippi walked out in protest.

Speaking on behalf of the MFDP, Bob Moses and Fannie Lou Hamer also rejected the settlement. Hamer, a Mississippi share-cropper and another indomitable woman activist, won over the hearts and minds of many with her eloquence in her appearances on network television. The Convention itself proceeded to a peaceful conclusion, but the incident intensified the sense of disillusionment of many SNCC activists with the Johnson administration. Divisions within the civil rights coalition were also deepened.

By 1964 problems had equally become apparent within the leadership ranks of southern white segregationists. The middle class-dominated Citizens' Councils, set up throughout the South between 1954 and 1959, were increasingly ineffective in resisting the drift towards desegregation. In consequence white southerners turned to more hard-line populist spokesmen. In 1962 George Wallace was elected Governor of Alabama with the uncompromising pledge to 'draw a line in the dust' and uphold 'segregation now, segregation tomorrow, segregation forever'. Diehard segregationists were similarly elected to the governorships of other southern states, including Orval Faubus in Arkansas, Ross Barnett in Mississippi and Lester Maddox in Georgia.

An even more disturbing development was a revival of the Ku Klux Klan in the South between 1959 and 1965, resulting in a series of violent outrages. In May 1961, Klansmen were involved in the brutal beatings of freedom riders in Birmingham, Alabama. In the summer of 1963 a Klan bombing campaign in the same city culminated in the death of five black schoolgirls at the Sixteenth Street Baptist Church on 15 September.

In neighbouring Mississippi, Klan leader Samuel Holloway Bowers targeted civil rights workers for assassination. Between 1964 and 1969 the Mississippi Klan was responsible for at least nine murders, 75 bombings and over 300 beatings. In the most notorious of these incidents, three civil rights activists, James Chaney, Andrew Goodman and Michael Schwerner, were murdered near the town of Philadelphia in Neshoba county.

Ultimately such outrages proved self-defeating. Within the South moderate segregationists and conservative businessmen were alienated by the rhetoric and actions of racial hard-liners. In April and May 1963 changes in the structure of the city government in Birmingham, Alabama, succeeded in removing the intemperate 'Bull' Conner from office. Similarly, in May 1963, the 'Big Mules', a group of influential businessmen in the city, brokered the private-sector peace agreement with Martin Luther King that ended the increasingly ugly racial confrontations in the city.

In the northern states, many whites previously apathetic towards racial injustice in the South were horrified by repeated scenes of police violence against peaceful civil rights protesters. Significantly, the major civil rights campaigns of the 1950s and 1960s coincided with the arrival of network television. In 1951 only 12 per cent of US homes had television sets, but this rose rapidly to 67 per cent by 1955, 90 per cent in 1963 and 95 per cent by 1968. Nightly news reports enabled northern and international audiences to witness for the first time the beating of non-violent civil rights protesters by segregationist law-enforcement officers. The 'American Dilemma' noted by Gunnar Myrdal in 1944 – the high-minded aspirations of the Declaration of Independence and US Constitution and the exclusion of blacks from them – had never been so graphically highlighted. This was a major factor in winning over public support for civil rights legislation and federal government intervention in the South.

# CHAPTER FOUR

# An African American summer
## Black Power, 1965–76

Despite the advances made between 1955 and 1965, racial relations remained an acute problem in US society, not least in the large cities of the North and on the West Coast, which had been left largely untouched by the campaigns of the civil rights movement. This neglect was highlighted by a major race riot in the Watts ghetto, a black residential area of Los Angeles in California, between 11 and 15 August 1965. Thirty-four people were killed, more than 1,000 injured and over $40 million lost in property damage, largely to white-owned businesses. Almost 3,500 rioters and looters were arrested. Disturbing enough in itself, Watts was one of the first of 239 outbreaks of racial violence in over 200 US cities in the five 'long hot summers' of 1964–8. Almost every large American city outside of the South was at some stage affected, including Oakland in California, 1965 and 1966, Cleveland, Ohio, 1966 and 1968, Chicago, Illinois, 1966 and 1968, Newark, New Jersey, 1967 and Detroit, Michigan, in 1967. The number and intensity of the riots, as well as their geographical diversity, also increased over time. In 1964 there were 16 serious outbreaks of violence in 16 cities, but the first five months of 1968 alone saw 65 riots in 64 cities. Between 1964 and 1972 inner-city ghetto riots resulted in at least 250 deaths, 10,000 serious injuries and 60,000 arrests. Incalculable millions of dollars were lost in damage to shops and businesses. This reflected the fact that the anger and frustration of ghetto residents were directed primarily against property rather than people. The majority of fatalities resulted from shootings by local police forces and national guardsmen rather than directly from the actions of rioters themselves.

In the aftermath of the violence a myriad of *ad hoc* riot commissions were set up by city, state and federal authorities to identify the
causes of urban disorders and to suggest effective remedies. The most
famous of these was the Kerner Commission, or National Advisory
Commission on Civil Disorders, created by President Lyndon
Johnson on 29 July 1967. The Kerner Report, published in February
1968, and running to several hundred pages, highlighted the
extent of social and economic deprivation in many black ghetto
communities. The Commission called for sweeping reforms in
employment, education, welfare, housing, and law enforcement.

In its early years the Johnson administration was committed to
expanding Kennedy's 'New Frontier' by a further series of social,
economic and welfare initiatives collectively known as the 'Great
Society'. Community Action Programmes (CAPs) were established at
local level across the nation in an attempt to overcome poverty and
social injustice. The financing of these measures led to increased tax
burdens on the middle class. Moreover, by 1968, a presidential
election year, the escalating cost of the Vietnam War, then at its
height, was accounting for an ever-larger proportion of federal
government expenditure. In this climate there was little political
will within the administration to engage in costly new initiatives, and
the main recommendations of the Kerner Report were effectively
shelved.

This was the general fate of most riot commission reports.
The commissions were set up in the immediate aftermath of urban
disorders; their prime function was often to provide reassurance
to anxious voters and to restore a climate of normality. Any sense
of urgency, or recognition of a need for reform, had usually long
since evaporated by the time riot commission reports were published
several months later. Often riot investigation agencies did not
demand such measures, but rather sought to shift the responsibility
for events to elsewhere in the political structure. City riot commissions thus sought to highlight the neglect and inattention of state
administrations. State investigations were critical of local municipal
authorities and the federal government.

Conservative politicians, city officials and local police chiefs often
blamed the personal inadequacies of rioters themselves for urban
disorders. Outbreaks of violence were thus attributed to rebellious
teenagers – 'wild youngsters' – outside agitators and criminal
elements, or recent migrants to the city who were unaccustomed to

urban life. Police records of those arrested presented a different picture. Although most rioters were male, they were usually long-term ghetto residents, without prior criminal convictions, from all sections of black ghetto society, and often in their twenties or thirties.

The actual causes of urban conflict were more deep-seated and complex than the character failings of a few individuals. Despite the Great Society programmes, levels of economic deprivation were high in many inner-city neighbourhoods. Growing factory automation led to the loss of many unskilled jobs in the 1950s and 1960s, a trend which disproportionately affected black communities. In 1962 46 per cent of the long-term unemployed (over 15 weeks) in the United States were black. Among black teenagers, and in particular cities, the statistics were even worse. Some city districts, as in Chicago, had 50–70 per cent black youth unemployment.

Standards of education in the ghetto were typically bad, with poorer physical facilities, larger class sizes and less-qualified teachers provided for black children than their white suburban counterparts. In the early 1960s only 32 per cent of black ghetto pupils completed high school compared to 56 per cent of white children.

Relations between local police forces and black communities were a longstanding source of grievance in many cities. Law-enforcement officers were almost always white and not residents of the ghettos that they patrolled. This, in conjunction with the aggressive preventative policing tactics that officers often employed, resulted in frequent instances of police shootings and brutality against ghetto residents. In many riots the initial violence was ignited by a confrontational incident involving the police and local blacks.

Although poor living conditions were not a new feature of ghetto life in the 1960s, they existed in a climate of rising expectations. The highly publicized campaigns of the civil rights movement raised both the hopes and the race consciousness of urban blacks. When aspirations were not met with any tangible gains, pent-up anger, frustration and despair all too often found release in semi-spontaneous acts of violence directed against property and authority. In this sense rioting represented less a form of violent intimidation than a desperate call for help and recognition.

Urban disorders revealed the extent to which civil rights campaigns, focused on ending segregation and discrimination, had failed to confront problems of poverty and economic inequality.

Between 1965 and 1968 all the leading civil rights organizations sought, in various ways, to meet this new challenge. In July and August 1966 Martin Luther King led an SCLC campaign in Chicago, its first initiative outside the South, to improve social conditions, employment opportunities, and education for blacks in the city. In a summit agreement of 26 August the municipal authorities and private-sector interests pledged themselves to end housing discrimination in the Windy City, but little was achieved in practice. The relative failure of the campaign reflected the lack of any prior SCLC organization in Chicago and the shrewd, albeit cynical, tactics employed by Mayor Richard Daley to minimize any concessions. Local whites in Chicago were also strongly, and at times violently, opposed to any changes in the status quo.

Despite this setback the Chicago campaign heralded a new development in King's philosophy. He increasingly stressed the need to fight economic injustice as well as racism. On 31 May 1967, in an SCLC staff retreat, King called for a radical redistribution of economic and political power. On 4 December he announced the launch of what was to be his last major initiative, a 'Poor People's Campaign' for the following year. The venture sought to create a coalition of the disadvantaged of all races. It culminated in a series of protests and rallies in Washington, DC from 11 May to 19 June 1968, participants staying in 'Resurrection City', an encampment near the Washington monument. Once again the campaign failed to result in any gains, and the SCLC was left with a $71,000 bill from the National Parks Department for clearing up the debris and remains of Resurrection City. Events in Washington were also overshadowed by the death of Martin Luther King. King was assassinated in Memphis, Tennessee, on 4 April 1968, by a lone white gunman, James Earl Ray, after going to the city to support a strike by black sanitation workers.

The issue of poverty and the geographical shift in civil rights activity to the cities of the North were reflected in policy changes made by CORE during the mid-1960s. In October 1964, James Farmer, National Director of CORE, introduced a new economics department within the organization to promote local neighbourhood action to develop black producer and consumer cooperatives. CORE 'Freedom Houses' were established in ghetto communities to provide information and counselling on employment, housing, health, education and a range of other issues. Following the passage of

Lyndon Johnson's 1964 War on Poverty Act many CORE workers, along with other civil rights activists, took up employment with federal CAPs set up to help communities overcome poverty. The focus on urban problems brought a higher public profile for the National Urban League, the smallest of the five leading civil rights organizations. In April 1968 Whitney Young, Executive Director of the NUL 1961–1971, launched 'New Thrust', an initiative aimed at developing economic self-help in ghetto communities. In February 1971 'Federal Thrust', introduced by the Republican administration of President Richard Nixon, committed $28 million in federal aid to the League for social and economic projects.

The external events of the Vietnam War provided civil rights organizations with a challenge of a different sort. The first major public protest against the war took place on 17 April 1965 in Washington, DC. Although it was organized by a mainly white radical group, Students for a Democratic Society (SDS), the executive committee of the SNCC also supported the event. Bob Moses, one of the best-known figures within the SNCC, spoke at the rally and sought to enlist the support of civil rights activists against the war. In July 1966, the annual convention of CORE, meeting in Baltimore, also passed an anti-war resolution. In sharp contrast, the NAACP and the NUL, the most conservative of the major civil rights organizations, maintained a policy of public support for the war effort.

These different responses to the Vietnam War widened the already growing divisions within the coalition of civil rights organizations and presented a painful personal dilemma for Martin Luther King. By early 1965 King was troubled increasingly by the moral issues raised by the US intervention in Vietnam. He did not voice these doubts in public for fear of alienating the Johnson administration and more conservative civil rights leaders like Roy Wilkins, Whitney Young and Philip Randolph, who all supported the war. On 4 April 1967, however, disturbed by reports of civilian suffering in the conflict, particularly that of children, King made a strong anti-war speech, 'Beyond Vietnam', in New York City.

King's public identification with the anti-war movement, combined with his growing stress of economic issues, has led some commentators to conclude that he was going through a process of radicalization during the last three years of his life. Although there is some justification for this view, it should be noted that the central components of his philosophy remained unchanged. King was stead-fast in his commitment to non-violence and, in 1966, opposed the use of the slogan 'Black Power' because of its anti-white connotations. King's most deeply held convictions were derived from his Baptist upbringing and theological studies. Since his days at Crozer he was committed to the concept of the 'Social Gospel', the belief that church ministers should be actively involved in social and economic issues. Both at Crozer and the University of Boston he was influenced by the teachings of 'Personalism', a school of religious thought that stressed the innate importance of every human individual and the ability of each person to have a direct relationship with God.

In a personal religious experience during the Montgomery bus boycott, on 27 January 1956, King became convinced that his role within the campaign was the result of divine will. The historian and journalist David Garrow has argued that this gave to King a sense of Christian mission which he retained for the rest of his life. On this interpretation the personal trials and tribulations endured by Martin Luther King were an act of religious faith, a part of the duty of all Christians to 'bear the Cross' in their daily lives. It was not unnatural that this sense of purpose, initially directed against segregation, should later have led King to speak out against poverty and war.

In addition to the war in Vietnam the unity of the civil rights movement was also threatened by internal developments within the main civil rights organizations. Between 1963 and 1965 the growing political and social radicalization of the SNCC, and to a lesser extent CORE, created tensions with older, more established, civil rights campaigners. Younger activists were alienated by the religiosity of church leaders and tired of the unquestioned commitment to non-violence. The celebrity status accorded to Martin Luther King, nicknamed 'de great lawd' by SNCC workers, came to be a source of irritation. This was more than just petty jealousy: it was believed that the hierarchical style of leadership associated with King stifled democracy and initiative at local level.

Racial divisions also began to emerge. Initially white volunteers had been welcomed within SNCC and CORE, but, over time, they became a source of resentment among black co-workers. Articulate and well educated, white activists often assumed a dominant role in local leadership and organization. It was inevitable that, ultimately, growing confidence and success would lead black civil rights workers to believe that they should take control of their own organizations. Added resentment was created by the high-profile media coverage of segregationist violence against white activists when the same acts of brutality against blacks often went unreported. Some black activists also came to question the long-term commitment of white volunteers to the movement. Civil rights were perceived to be a faddish affectation among white students, a fashion trend which could change at any time. Summing up this mood, the radical black SNCC leader Stokely Carmichael dubbed white volunteers the 'Pepsi Generation', getting high on civil rights.

Inner tensions within the civil rights movement coincided with the emergence of more militant black spokespersons, both within the United States and in the wider international community. Beginning with Ghana in 1957, national liberation movements in Africa started to achieve independence from white colonial rule. African leaders, like Nkrumah in Ghana, became influential role models for black civil rights activists within America. Often Third World revolutionaries advocated armed resistance to colonial rule, which contrasted with the non-violent philosophy of the civil rights movement. In his influential work *The Wretched of the Earth* (1961), first published in an English translation in 1965, Frantz Fanon, an Algerian nationalist born in Martinique, wrote of the 'cleansing force of violence'.

Radical black nationalists within the United States also commanded public attention. Following the decline of Garveyism in the late 1920s the most important black nationalist organization was the Black Muslim movement or Nation of Islam (NOI). The Nation was originally founded in 1930, in Detroit, by W. D. Fard, an enigmatic mystic of whom little is known. Following Fard's mysterious disappearance in March 1934, leadership of the sect fell to Elijah Muhammed. Born in Georgia in 1897, as Elijah Poole, Muhammed was the son of ex-slaves. He led the NOI from 1934 until his death in 1975, claiming to be the prophet of Allah and assuming the title 'Messenger of Islam'.

Despite frequent links and contacts with the Muslim world, the theology of the NOI differed in important respects from traditional Islamic beliefs. Elijah Muhammed's teachings denied the possibility of any resurrection or spiritual rebirth after death. He instructed followers that only the black race was the original creation of Allah. All other races were not of divine origin but the result of a series of genetic experiments by an evil black scientist, Yacub. The last, and most depraved, of Yacub's creations was the white race. These 'blue-eyed devils' were the natural enemy of all black people. Black Muslims were therefore commanded to minimize all social contacts with whites and racial intermarriage was strictly prohibited. Whites would rule the world for 6,000 years but would then be destroyed in a divine holocaust that would occur at some unspecified date before the year 2000. Allah himself would appear in a giant warplane, or starship, in the sky. Unusual weather phenomena or plane crashes were often viewed as divine portents of this day of judgement.

Between the 1930s and the 1950s the Nation was a little-known organization. Elijah Muhammed concentrated on developing NOI temples in the black ghettos of the North, in cities like Detroit, New York and Chicago. The Nation had a low profile outside these areas. This changed dramatically in 1959 as a result of a television documentary, *The Hate that Hate Produced*, made by a white journalist, Michael Wallace, and his black colleague, Louis Lomax. In a series of five half-hour programmes the documentary looked at the religious beliefs of the Nation. Excerpts were shown from a play, *The Trial*, written by NOI minister Louis X, later to be better known as Louis Farrakhan. In this theatrical production a white man was tried and sentenced to death by a black judge and jury for the crimes of the white race. *The Hate that Hate Produced* gave the NOI instant national recognition and notoriety.

NOI membership reached 65,000 to 100,000 by 1960 and some 250,000 by 1969. The Nation also enjoyed considerable influence and respect in the wider black community, with its official newspaper *Muhammed Speaks* enjoying a weekly circulation of 600,000 by the early to mid-1970s. Both in his writings and in his public appearances Elijah Muhammed deliberately cultivated an aura of mystery and mystique, making the Nation a source of fascination for many African Americans.

Black ghetto dwellers were attracted to the NOI by its stress on racial pride and economic self-help. Putting principle into practice, Elijah Muhammed and his son Wallace Muhammed created a range of Black Muslim businesses, including restaurants, bakeries and grocery stores. Symbols of the organization's success, these enterprises also provided employment for NOI members in northern black ghetto communities where job opportunities were usually scarce. Converts to the Nation were expected to donate 10 per cent of their earnings to the sect, and to adopt an austere personal lifestyle requiring total abstinence from alcohol and tobacco, prayers five times a day, and conservative clothing – long dresses for women and distinctive dark suits and bow ties for men.

The NOI was particularly successful in winning converts among African Americans on the margins of society, like alcoholics, drug addicts, criminals and prison inmates. Malcolm X, who was to become the Nation's most influential and successful national spokesman in the early 1960s, was recruited in jail.

Born as Malcolm Little in Omaha, Nebraska, on 19 May 1925, Malcolm X had a troubled childhood. His father, Earl Little, an ardent Garveyite and Baptist minister, was run over and killed by a tram car in 1931. This was treated by the authorities as no more than a tragic accident, but unexplained circumstances surrounding the incident led family members to believe that he had been murdered by a white supremacist organization, the Black Legion. Following her husband's death Malcolm's mother, Louise Little, was left to bring up eight children on her own during the height of the Great Depression. The family endured extreme hardship and were forced to rely on humiliating means-tested welfare benefits. In 1937 the stress of this existence led to Louise Little suffering a mental break-down. The 12-year-old Malcolm was temporarily fostered out to a white family, the Swerlins. In his autobiography the adult Malcolm X recalled how the foster family had treated him in a patronizing manner and as a racial inferior. Similar experiences at the hands of white school teachers left him deeply cynical about the prospects for genuine racial integration within the United States.

In 1941 Malcolm dropped out of high school and went to live with his sister in Roxbury, the black ghetto district of Boston. During the Second World War he passed through a succession of jobs which included being a shoeshine boy and a railway dining-car attendant on the Boston to New York route. At this time he was drawn increasingly into a life of drug dealing and petty crime, earning the nickname 'Detroit Red'. In 1945 his criminal career came to an abrupt end when he was arrested for house-breaking in Boston. Duly tried and convicted, he was sentenced to 10 years' imprisonment, despite being only 21 years of age and with no prior criminal record. A contributing factor in the severity of this sentence was the outrage of the trial judge at Malcolm's sexual relationship with a white woman who was one of the co-defendants.

In jail Malcolm first encountered the Nation of Islam and even entered into a personal correspondence with Elijah Muhammed. After his release from prison in 1952 Malcolm became a full convert to the Nation. Enjoying the favour of Elijah Muhammed, he rose rapidly within the organization, becoming the minister of Temple No. 7 in Harlem in 1954. He built up a strong personal following among ghetto blacks with his charismatic personality and scathing denunciations of white America and mainstream civil rights leaders. In 1959 Malcolm X, as he was now known, featured prominently in the Wallace and Lomax television documentary.

Between 1959 and 1965 he commanded national and international recognition as a black spokesperson. Within the United States he was a regular speaker on the college lecture circuit and made frequent appearances on network television. In these years Malcolm X acted as a militant counterpoint to Martin Luther King, rejecting integration with whites and voicing the anger and frustration of the black ghetto underclass.

More than just a national spokesman for the NOI, Malcolm X developed into an independent thinker and commentator in his own right. This transformation led to increasingly strained relations with Elijah Muhammed, who viewed him as a challenge to his own authority within the Nation. Conversely, media revelations about Muhammed's lavish lifestyle, and his extramarital affairs, undermined Malcolm X's faith in the 'Messenger of Islam'. On policy issues Malcolm X doubted the wisdom of the Nation's strategy of strict non-involvement in civil rights campaigns. He also sought to develop closer links with mainstream Islam, which led to him questioning the Nation's unorthodox beliefs.

Theses various sources of tension reached a crisis point in November 1963 when, in the aftermath of the assassination of President Kennedy, Malcolm X publicly observed that 'it was . . . a case of the chickens coming home to roost'. The racial hatred of whites 'had not stopped with the killing of defenseless black people, but that hate, allowed to spread unchecked, finally had struck down this country's chief of state'. This statement directly contravened an instruction from Elijah Muhammed to NOI spokespersons to make no public comment on the assassination. By way of censure he suspended Malcolm X from the Nation for a period of 90 days. Although he initially accepted this punishment, the suspension effectively marked Malcolm X's final break with the NOI.

Early in 1964 he issued a declaration of independence and established his own spiritual headquarters in New York City, the Muslim Mosque. This was followed by a pilgrimage, or *haji*, to Mecca, a visit to Africa, and meetings with black African leaders. On his return to the United States in June Malcolm X founded the Organization of Afro-American Unity (OAAU). The stated objectives of the OAAU were to unify all peoples of African descent and to promote political, social and economic independence for blacks. In the event, Malcolm X had little opportunity to reach these ambitious goals. Speaking at the Audubon ballroom in Harlem, on 21 February 1965, he was shot dead by gunmen from the NOI.

The contribution and achievements of Malcolm X as a race leader have been a subject of controversy. In a famous 1965 article, 'The Ambiguous Legacy of Malcolm X', Tom Kahn and Bayard Rustin put forward the views of some civil rights leaders in depicting him as little more than an irresponsible media personality. A fierce critic of the major civil rights organizations, Malcolm X was never able to develop any mass organization of his own or fully advance any alternative programme for racial progress.

In contrast to the practical initiatives of Martin Luther King, Malcolm X's achievements were of a more abstract and philosophical nature. He highlighted the limitations of the civil rights movement, most notably its failure to remedy economic deprivation in northern black ghetto communities. More than any other African American spokesperson of his day he was responsible for the international-ization of black protest, linking the struggle of American blacks with that of Third World independence movements. He was a major source of inspiration to leaders of the emerging Black Power movement in the United States in the late 1960s. In the 1980s and 1990s Malcolm X remained an icon and role model for successive generations of young African Americans, particularly in the ghettos. Central to his intellectual legacy was *The Autobiography of Malcolm X* (1965), an account of his life dictated by Malcolm X to the black journalist Alex Haley. A powerful narrative account of his search for spiritual fulfilment and racial self-enlightenment, the *Autobiography* was arguably Malcolm X's greatest achievement.

The philosophy and ideas of Malcolm X have been much debated. During the last 16 months of his life Malcolm X's thoughts and beliefs went through a process of rapid change, and they were still in a state of flux at the time of his death. In this period he embraced orthodox Islam and abandoned his earlier blanket rejection of all whites as 'blue-eyed devils'. Deeply moved by the interracial harmony of fellow Muslims on his 1964 *haji*, he no longer denied the possibility of integration, accepting, for example, the idea of interracial marriage. At the same time Malcolm X showed a growing sympathy for Third World socialism and rejected capitalist values. This has led some commentators, most notably George Breitman, to argue that Malcolm X had become a socialist revolutionary in the last months of his life.

It should, however, be noted that Malcolm X made no firm commitment to any class-based liberation strategy. Writers such as Albert Cleage and Benjamin Karim have therefore claimed that he remained essentially a black nationalist who believed in racial separation. Adopting a more general interpretive framework, historians James Cone and Peter Goldman have viewed Malcolm X more as a public moralist, a voice of conscience who drew attention to the nation's social and racial ills. Biographers Eugene Wolfenstein and Bruce Perry have adopted a psycho-historical approach. From this perspective Malcolm X's ideas and thoughts are viewed in the context of his personal psychological development. His beliefs as an adult are seen as having been shaped by his traumatic childhood and his experiences and consciousness as a member of a racially oppressed minority.

The example of Malcolm X and black African independence movements had a profound impact on the younger generation of black leaders within the civil rights movement, particularly in the SNCC and CORE. A growing sense of militancy led to the election of the 24-year-old Stokely Carmichael as Chairman of the SNCC in 1966, replacing John Lewis. In January 1966 the radical Floyd McKissick was elected as National Director of CORE, filling the vacancy created by the resignation of James Farmer in December 1965.

Divisions between the SNCC, CORE and the more conservative SCLC, NAACP and NUL were publicly highlighted in the Mississippi 'March Against Fear', in June 1966. The march was originally a lone initiative of James Meredith, who in 1962 had been the first black student to be admitted to the University of Mississippi. Three days into the protest Meredith was injured by a sniper and unable to continue. In a symbolic act of unity, Martin Luther King, Carmichael and McKissick agreed to continue the march on Meredith's behalf. A spontaneous gesture, the new march suffered from a lack of preplanning and organization. Wary of the radical McKissick and Carmichael, NAACP Executive Secretary Roy Wilkins declined to commit any representative to the march. During its early stages the non-violent King objected to the presence of armed black guards from the Louisiana 'Deacons of Defense'. On 16 June Stokely Carmichael was arrested by the local police authorities. In a public interview, following his release six hours later, he called for the achievement of 'Black Power'. Although it had been used before, the incident marked the first popular adoption of the phrase, which was also taken up by McKissick. The term 'Black Power' acquired added significance when King threatened to withdraw from the march because of the slogan's violent and anti-white connotations. In the event harmony was restored and the protest reached a successful conclusion at the state capital, Jackson, on 26 June.

Despite this semblance of unity, the divisions brought to the surface by the concept of Black Power remained. In July 1966 the annual CORE convention, meeting in Baltimore, Maryland, endorsed the idea of Black Power. A resolution was passed against the Vietnam War and the organization's commitment to non-violence was qualified by the passage of a motion that supported the right of blacks to armed self-defence. In August 1966 CORE's headquarters were relocated from Chicago to Harlem. The 1967 annual convention deleted the word 'multiracial' from CORE's constitution, and by the summer of 1968 whites were officially excluded from active membership within the organization. In September the same year McKissick resigned as CORE National Director and was replaced by the more militant Roy Innis.

Developments within the SNCC were even more dramatic. In a special meeting in New York City in December 1966, the SNCC's ten-member Central Committee voted to expel all whites from the organization. In May 1967, at the annual meeting of SNCC staff in Atlanta, Stokely Carmichael was replaced as SNCC Chairman by Henry 'Rap' Brown, a radical and controversial advocate of black armed self-defence. The meeting also affirmed the SNCC's support for 'libertarian struggles against colonialism, racism and economic exploitation' throughout the world.

Living up to his reputation, on 25 July 1967 Rap Brown delivered a highly provocative 40-minute speech to blacks in Cambridge, Maryland. The address called on African Americans to take over white-owned stores in the ghetto, if necessary by violence and arson.

Shortly after the rally a race riot broke out in the city. Blacks and police engaged in a shoot-out in which Brown was wounded. At another rally in Oakland, California, on 17 February 1968, the SNCC entered into a public alliance with the revolutionary organization the Black Panthers.

One of the most radical of all Black Power groups, the Black Panther Party for Self-Defense was founded in Oakland, California in October 1966 by Huey Newton, aged 24, and Bobby Seale, aged 30. In ideological terms Newton and Seale were strongly influenced by Malcolm X and Third World revolutionaries like Che Guevara, Frantz Fanon and Mao Tse-tung. The principal demands of the Panthers were incorporated into a ten-point manifesto. The manifesto was nationalistic in tone; individual aims in it included: a payment of reparations to African Americans by the federal government, as compensation for slavery; an exemption of blacks from military service; and freedom for blacks held in federal, state, county and city prisons or jails, unless tried and convicted by a jury of their peers from within the black community. The separatist thinking of the Panthers was implied, though not fully spelt out, in point ten, their 'major political objective' of a United Nations referendum of 'black colonial subjects' in the United States 'for the purpose of determining the will of black people as to their national destiny'.

Between 1967 and 1970 this nationalistic agenda gave way to a vision of a class-based revolutionary struggle aimed at mobilizing the lumpenproletariat. The Panthers sought to develop links with Third World liberation movements in Africa, Asia and South America. Within the United States they cultivated links not just with the SNCC but other minority groups, including the Mexican 'Brown Berets', the Puerto Rican 'Young Lords' and the Chinese American 'Red Guards'. Alliances were also developed with radical white-dominated organizations.

Membership of the Black Panthers never surpassed 5,000 people. It was largely confined to some 30 chapters in urban centres on the West Coast, like Oakland, and the major cities of the North, including Boston, Chicago and New York. Nonetheless, the Panthers commanded a widespread admiration and respect in black ghetto communities that belied their lack of numerical strength. Support for the Panthers derived less from their political ideology than their stress on practical self-help. In 1968 and 1969 the Panthers introduced a 'Breakfasts for Children' programme in major black ghettos across the country to counter the inadequate diet of many black inner-city pupils. Panther clinics were set up in ghettos to provide free advice on health, welfare and legal rights. A people's free clothing programme was also introduced.

More controversially, the Panthers undertook to monitor levels of police brutality and the harassment of black communities by law-enforcement officers. They also adopted a paramilitary style uniform of black berets, pale blue shirts, black leather jackets and black trousers and shoes. A liberal interpretation was placed on the right to carry arms as defined in the second amendment to the US Constitution. Party members appeared heavily armed in public and Panther patrols followed police cars around the ghetto. This resulted in tense relations with law-enforcement agencies and, in some instances, violent shoot-outs.

There is considerable evidence to suggest that Panther activists were the targets of systematic police persecution. At the same time, many Panthers were recruited from prisons and had a past history of violence. This applied to both Huey Newton and Eldridge Cleaver, who emerged as the third major leader of the party. Details of Cleaver's early life were recorded in a controversial series of autobiographical essays, *Soul on Ice* (1967). This work was written whilst Cleaver was serving time in prison as a serial rapist. Cleaver had initially justified his crimes as an 'insurrectionary act' that defiled and trampled upon the 'white man's law' by 'defiling his women'. He subsequently repudiated this violent past and was released from jail in December 1966.

The internal organization of the Panthers was centralized and hierarchical. The party's key decision-making body was a non-elected National Central Committee. This effectively comprised a shadow revolutionary government with Huey Newton as Minister of Defense, Bobby Seale as Central Committee Chairman and Eldridge Cleaver as Minister of Information. Other important figures on the committee included Cleaver's wife Kathleen, Communications Secretary; David Hilliard, Chief of Staff; Don Cox, Field Marshal; Roy Hewitt, Minister of Education; and Emory Douglas, Minister of Culture. Following the alliance with the SNCC, in February 1968, Stokely Carmichael was appointed to the National Central Committee as Prime Minister, James Forman of SNCC was made Minister of Foreign Affairs, and Rap Brown became Minister of Justice. This show of unity did not last long. Forman and Brown both resigned from the committee by the end of the year. In July 1969 Carmichael also departed and the SNCC's Central Committee voted to end the alliance with the Panthers.

The rift was partly the result of personality differences, but the main reason for it was ideological. Under the leadership of Carmichael and Brown the SNCC was, at least in the short term, committed to a separatist black nationalist programme. This conflicted with the movement of the Panthers towards a multi-racial class-based struggle. This polarization between black nationalism and the vision of a proletarian revolution constituted an important philosophical division within the wider Black Power movement.

The nationalist perspective was most clearly articulated by Stokely Carmichael and Charles Hamilton in their 1967 book, *Black Power: The Politics of Liberation*. In this work Carmichael and Hamilton saw the problems experienced by African Americans in terms of colonial oppression. Third World nations were the victims of 'external colonialism', invasion by an imperial European power followed by political and economic exploitation. Within the United States, black Americans were the victims of 'internal colonialism'. Police forces patrolled the ghetto like an army of occupation and whites had a near monopoly of political and economic power. White-owned ghetto businesses, rather than reinvesting profits in the local community, exported wealth to the more affluent suburbs. At the same time white-run banks, financial institutions and real estate agents denied potential black entrepreneurs the necessary capital to challenge this economic hegemony. In seeking a remedy blacks could not therefore enter into alliances with white politicians and white-run organizations, for these were part of the system of colonial oppression. Instead, blacks should seek to develop alliances with Third World liberation movements in a common struggle against imperialism. To this end, during 1966 and 1967 Carmichael and other SNCC activists visited, amongst other nations, Cuba, North Vietnam, the Soviet Union, China and Guinea.

Within America Carmichael advocated economic self-help programmes and support for independent black candidates for elective office. In April 1966 the SNCC helped to establish the all-black political party, the Lowndes County Freedom Organization (LCFO) in Alabama. The party's logo, a black panther, was adopted by Bobby Seale and Huey Newton for their Black Panther Party for Self-Defense in California.

The nationalist perspective of Carmichael and the class-based ideology of the Black Panthers were only two of a variety of differing interpretations of Black Power in the late 1960s. An important strength and weakness of the Black Power movement was its multi-faceted nature. Young, well-educated black activists within the movement were inclined to be 'cosmopolitans', attracted by ideas of internationalism and familiar with the writings of Third World leaders like Fanon and Mao. Older, less-educated blacks, in the ghetto or the rural South, were attracted by practical grassroots programmes set up to achieve community empowerment. In this spirit a Black Power labour organization, the Dodge Revolutionary Union Movement (DRUM), was established by black workers at the Chrysler car plant in Michigan in May 1968. This was followed by the formation of the Ford Revolutionary Union Movement (FRUM) and the General Motors Revolutionary Union Movement (GRUM). In 1969 these various groups united in an umbrella Black Power union, the League of Revolutionary Workers (LRW).

At the same time as the LRW called for more workers' rights, a conservative black Republican, Nathan Wright, put forward a vision of Black Power as black capitalism. To this end he organized conferences of black professionals and businessmen in Newark, New Jersey, in July 1967, and Philadelphia, Pennsylvania in June 1968. The latter event was sponsored by the white Clairol Corporation, with the company's president a keynote speaker at the conference. This interpretation of Black Power was sufficiently conservative to win over the endorsement of the most right-wing politicians and organizations. In this vein, in July 1968 the NUL and the SCLC annual convention in August both approved the concept of Black Power. Black Power as black capitalism even won the enthusiastic backing of Republican candidate Richard Nixon in his 1968 presidential election campaign.

One of the few areas in which most Black Power advocates could agree was the need for greater emphasis on black pride and black culture. Seeking to rediscover their African roots many young black Americans adopted Afro-style haircuts and African dress. In colleges and universities African American students successfully campaigned for the introduction of black studies programmes, and for greater emphasis on black history and black literature in existing courses. In Los Angeles the United Slaves (US) organization of Maulenga Ron Karenga adopted African cultural forms. One of Karenga's leading supporters, the black poet Amiri Baraka (formerly known as Le Roi Jones), helped to inspire the Black Arts movement.

The diverse and sometimes conflicting nature of the Black Power movement was highlighted by the fact that Karenga's followers were often involved in heated confrontations with Black Panther activists. Supportive of black cultural and black studies programmes in principle, the Panthers disagreed with the US organization on how far these should be pursued and their overall importance. The Panthers believed that at best overemphasis on cultural, or 'pork chop', nationalism was a time-wasting irrelevancy. Adoption of African lifestyles distracted attention from the need to achieve political and economic change. At worst, excessive cultural pride could be reactionary and racist, as embodied in the despotic 'Papa Doc' Duvalier regime in Haiti.

In terms of popular culture, the campaigns of the civil rights movement and the emergence of Black Power were reflected in a variety of different ways during the 1950s and 1960s. After the Second World War there was a major expansion in the number of radio stations and programmes targeted on black listeners. The growth of urban black communities meant that large black audiences could be reached by small local operators. At the same time the loss of white listeners to the new medium of television meant that radio stations, albeit still largely white owned and funded, sought to compensate by targeting minority audiences.

Until the early 1950s African American music aired on radio played largely to black listeners. This changed dramatically in 1954–5 when black Rhythm and Blues records broke through into the white market, paving the way for the emergence of Rock and Roll. 'Crossover' artists such as Little Richard, Chuck Berry and Fats Domino became household names. Leading white performers, most famously Elvis Presley, openly imitated black musical styles and made cover versions of black records.

The reasons for this mainstreaming of black popular music were complex. In part they reflected the move towards integration ushered in by the *Brown* decision and the Montgomery bus boycott. Less positively, the appeal of black performers derived from stereotyped beliefs that African Americans possessed natural rhythm and that they were physically and sexually uninhibited. White teenagers also played R and B and Rock and Roll music because of its controversial image and ability to shock parents. In the late 1950s conservative national and state politicians, particularly in the South, engaged in a verbal tirade against the Rock and Roll phenomenon. It was denounced variously as injurious to mental health, a cause of juvenile delinquency and sexually obscene. Rock and Roll concerts were frequently banned by city councils or became the scene of violent racial clashes. On 10 April 1956 even the impeccable black interracial diplomat Nat King Cole was attacked by white segregationists whilst on stage at the Municipal Auditorium in Birmingham, Alabama.

The assault on Cole was the more ironic because at the time, like most black musical performers, he was not actively involved in the civil rights struggle. Apart from the odd notable exception, such as Harry Belafonte, the best-known musical celebrities to support black civil rights openly were white performers such as Bob Dylan and Joan Baez. Dylan and Baez not only made financial contributions to the civil rights movement but also included political references in their songs. In 1963, for example, Dylan's *Oxford Town* was a direct commentary on the opposition to James Meredith's admission to the University of Mississippi in 1962.

The reluctance of black Rhythm and Blues and Rock and Roll artists to identify themselves publicly with the civil rights movement was partly for commercial reasons. Controversial civil rights activity might have resulted in a loss of sales to white record buyers. On a personal level, leading figures within the civil rights movement in the late 1950s and early 1960s made unlikely associates for Rock and Roll musicians. Conservative, middle-class, black churchmen did not fit comfortably into the hedonistic lifestyle of Rock and Roll celebrities. Martin Luther King himself had reservations about the morality of the new music.

The emergence of younger, more radical leaders, like Stokely Carmichael and Rap Brown, in the mid-1960s went some way to overcoming this image problem. Over time black artists felt a personal need to identify with the cause of black civil rights. This was witnessed by the release of *Mississippi Goddam* by Nina Simone in 1964, which coincided with the Mississippi Summer Project. The song became an unofficial anthem of young civil rights activists, rivalling the more conservative and religious *We Shall Overcome*.

The Black Power emphasis on racial pride and African culture created obvious commercial opportunities for black performers. This was highlighted by the rise of Soul music, most notably from the Tamla Motown corporation, established by Berry Gordy in 1959 in Detroit, which enjoyed enormous success between 1964 and 1967. Strongly influenced by black gospel music, Soul paradoxically reflected a growing secularization of the civil rights movement. Soul stars adapted gospel rhythms to their music, but without the religious connotations. In the late 1960s leading Soul performers frequently made recordings designed to demonstrate their political and racial awareness. In 1967 the release of *R-E-S-P-E-C-T* by Aretha Franklin, the 'Queen of Soul', was testimony to the new sense of black pride. Not to be outdone, the 'Grandfather of Soul', James Brown recorded *Soul Pride* and in 1968 sang *Say it Loud I'm Black and I'm Proud*. Soul music touched on political controversy as well as racial pride. In 1971 the album *There's a Riot Going On* by Sly and the Family Stone represented a sustained critique of US society. The Black Panthers even had their own Soul group, the Lumpen, who recorded their own material and wrote revolutionary new lyrics set to well-known tunes. *Old Man River* thus became transformed into *Old Pig Nixon*.

Black civil rights influenced Hollywood film in a variety of ways. In the 1950s and 1960s Sidney Poitier emerged as the first black Hollywood superstar and was the first African American to win an Oscar for best actor in *Lilies of the Field* (1963). Overall, however, film opportunities for black men remained limited and those for black women virtually non-existent. Even for Poitier the range of roles open to him was restricted. Many of his appearances were in contrived 'racially aware' films. In *The Defiant Ones* (1958) he played an escaped convict chained to a white fellow prisoner played by Tony Curtis. In *The Heat of the Night* (1967) he played a black New York City detective, Virgil Tibbs, investigating a murder in Mississippi for which, ironically, he was initially detained as a suspect by the local racist police chief, played by Rod Steiger.

'Mr Tibbs' typified a new Hollywood stereotype of the 1960s, dubbed by film historian Daniel Leab 'the ebony saint'. This character was usually middle class, and invariably intelligent, dignified and non-violent, often despite extreme provocation. Possessing no obvious personality flaws, he had a tolerance and understanding of the racist misconceptions of the whites who shared his environment. Saintliness had an added connotation in that the character usually had no visible sex life or desire to have one. Occasionally there were exceptions to this rule. *Island in the Sun* (1957) with Harry Belafonte and Poitier's *Guess Who's Coming to Dinner* (1967) both dealt with the subject of interracial sexual relationships. At the same time these productions were careful to show little actual physical intimacy between the lead characters. In *Guess Who's Coming to Dinner* the only on-screen kiss between Poitier and his white fiancée was seen by audiences as a reflection in the rear-view mirror of a taxi.

In box-office terms blacks were increasingly important to Hollywood by the 1960s. Although only about 13 per cent of the total US population, African Americans made up some 30 per cent of filmgoers in big cities, where the largest cinemas were located. Given that cinema was also youth-oriented, targeted mainly at the 15–25 age group, it was perhaps inevitable that filmmakers would seek to capitalize on the rise of Black Power, with its particular appeal to the younger generation of African Americans.

In the early 1970s a new film genre emerged, the 'blaxploitation' movie. In blaxploitation films all the leading characters were black, with whites confined to marginal roles or cast as corrupt, morally bankrupt adversaries to be overcome by the black star. The ebony saint gave way to the 'superspade', a strong, fearless black character, usually male, who not only triumphed over all enemies but also found time for serial sexual conquests of both black and white women. Violence and sexual encounters were typically portrayed in explicit detail. Aimed almost exclusively at black audiences, blaxploitation films were usually shot on minimal budgets. *Sweet Sweetback's Baadasssss Song* (1971), produced, directed and starring the black filmmaker Melvin Van Peebles, cost just $500,000 and was shot within three weeks but generated over $10,000,000 in income within a year of its release. The more ambitious MGM production *Shaft*, also shot in 1971, was made for $1,200,000 and grossed over $11,000,000 at the box office. *Sweet Sweetback's Baadasssss Song* and *Shaft* each acquired cult status, but most blaxploitation films were of poor quality with little artistic merit. Whereas Van Peebles sought to promote black pride, and what Malcolm X had called a 'decolonization of the black mind', many blaxploitation movies were little more than crude attempts to exploit the black market.

The emergence of television coincided almost exactly with the development of the civil rights movement. In the 1940s and 1950s, appearances by blacks on television were largely confined to occasional guest celebrities or news coverage of civil rights protests.

In 1952 black actors accounted for just 0.4 per cent of all television performances. The only commercially successful shows with blacks in starring roles had them portray comic racist stereotypes. In *Beulah* (1950–3), first Ethel Waters and then Louise Beavers played the part of a black housekeeper devoted to the white family who employed her. Worse still was CBS's *Amos 'n' Andy* (1951–3), a televised version of the 1930s radio hit, in which a now all-African American cast played grinning caricatures of lazy, ignorant blacks. Productions with more positive or challenging images of African Americans were unable to attract commercial sponsors or doomed to ratings failure by being scheduled in poor time slots. The *Nat King Cole Show* on NBC, which premiered on 5 November 1956, was cancelled within one season because of sponsorship problems. The controversial drama documentary series *East Side/West Side* (1963–4), which dealt with racial issues in several programmes, was abandoned after 26 episodes.

It was not until the second half of the 1960s that some qualified advances were finally achieved. In *Julia* (1968–71), Diahann Carroll played a successful young widowed nurse and mother. However, her character was criticized for being a 'white Negro', disconnected from African American culture and embodying white middle-class values. In *I, Spy* (1965–8), Bill Cosby co-starred with Robert Culp as two secret-service agents who worked together and bonded in interracial friendship. Blacks were also given co-starring or important supporting roles in many other successful series. In *Mission Impossible* (1966–73), Greg Morris played the electronics expert Barney Coleman. In *Ironside* (1967–75), Don Mitchell appeared as Mark Sanger, an aide and friend of the disabled chief detective played by Raymond Burr. Boldly going where few black women had been allowed to go before, Nichelle Nichols appeared as the attractive and intelligent communications officer on the bridge of the starship *Enterprise* in *Star Trek* (1966–9). Symbolically, the name of her character, Uhura, was derived from the Swahili word for freedom.

By 1970 Black Power had reached the peak of its success, but in the early 1970s the movement suffered a rapid decline. The reasons for this were many and complicated. The whole concept of Black Power was vague and the term never managed to achieve any precise meaning or definition. Initially, this was a source of strength, enabling a wide variety of groups to unite in support of a common slogan. In the longer term it was a major weakness as competing, and often irreconcilable, interests all sought to stamp their own interpretation on the movement. From 1967 onwards the leadership of the SNCC became increasingly preoccupied with ideological disputes between black separatists and class revolutionaries who advocated multi-racial alliances. The organization's practical grassroots initiatives in the South, the source of the SNCC's early successes, steadily declined in number. Internal dissension was matched by external discord. In July 1969 the short-lived alliance between the SNCC and the Black Panthers ended amid bitter public recriminations between Stokely Carmichael and Eldridge Cleaver.

Black Power was an appealing slogan that summed up the emotional feelings and sense of frustration experienced by African Americans in the late 1960s. Unfortunately, this was never translated into any well-thought-out practical programme for change. Class-based revolution, as envisaged by the Black Panthers, was manifestly out of touch with the realities of day-to-day life in the United States. The notion of internal colonialism advanced by Stokely Carmichael, although interesting as a concept, was, in practice, flawed and inconsistent. In the Third World the obvious solution to colonial oppression was for the majority indigenous population to expel the occupying colonial power and achieve national independence. This was clearly not the situation of black Americans, who were only a small minority of the US population and not the original inhabitants of the country. Significantly, Carmichael and Hamilton's book *Black Power* spent much time developing the theoretical notion of internal colonialism but offered little in the way of practical remedies.

Gender divisions were another source of weakness. In addition to Black Power the late 1960s saw the rise of the women's movement in the United States. Women volunteers, black and white, played an important part in civil rights protests during the 1950s and early 1960s. Experienced and motivated, many of these activists subsequently went on to campaign on behalf of feminist issues. Unfortunately, Black Power ideology contained strong elements of male chauvinism. Asked about the position of black women within the movement, Stokely Carmichael simply replied 'prone'. Although this answer may have offered more insight into Carmichael's sense of humour than his actual beliefs, it was a view that too many male Black Power activists genuinely shared. The superspade heroes of blaxploitation films typically treated women as little more than objects of sexual gratification. In real life, women activists, such as Elaine Brown of the Black Panthers, often encountered similar attitudes and found themselves relegated to secondary roles within Black Power organizations.

The exodus of white liberals from the civil rights movement represented the loss of another key constituency of support. All the major civil rights organizations were heavily dependent on financial donations from whites. In the late 1960s the perceived anti-white rhetoric of Black Power activists, and the expulsion of whites from the SNCC and CORE, had serious financial implications. The annual income of both the SNCC and CORE dropped sharply. In consequence, local grassroots projects had to be cut back, reinforcing the shift away from practical initiatives to arid ideological debate within the two organizations. By 1970 the SNCC had only three active chapters, in New York City, Atlanta, and Cincinnati, Ohio. It had no full-time employees, and the SNCC headquarters in New York City could not even afford a telephone. In December 1973 the SNCC ceased to exist as an organization. CORE avoided the same fate, but survived in a greatly truncated form.

For a variety of reasons the interest of white Americans in black issues declined in the late 1960s. The provocative actions and statements of Black Power spokespersons did not help, but the process of white disaffection with black civil rights was already underway by 1965–6. After ten years of constant campaigning and high-profile media attention civil rights issues no longer had such a dramatic impact. White television audiences began to experience 'compassion fatigue' concerning the problems of African Americans.

Initially northern whites sympathized with black civil rights campaigners because racial intolerance was perceived to be a largely southern problem. The urban ghetto riots of 1965–8 dispelled this comforting illusion. Racism was shown to be a complex, intractable national question that had no quick or easy answers. At the same time, by the mid-1960s civil rights campaigns shifted away from desegregation to issues of poverty and economic inequality. Improvements in the pay and employment prospects of blacks were seen as likely to threaten the job security and living standards of whites. Moreover, new issues, such as the Vietnam War and women's rights, emerged in the mid-1960s and shifted attention away from black civil rights. National political and media attention focused on these new topical questions. Difficult and still unresolved problems in race relations were consigned to the 'too hard' basket.

Changing attitudes towards black civil rights were reflected in the policies of the Republican administrations of President Richard Nixon, 1969–74. Nixon was a racial conservative by instinct, as were many of his leading aides, including Vice-President Spiro Agnew, Attorney General John Mitchell, and close political adviser John Ehrlichman. Political considerations reinforced Nixon's lukewarm attitude towards black civil rights. In the 1968 presidential election Nixon defeated the Democratic candidate, Hubert Humphrey, by the comparatively narrow margin of some 500,000 votes. The closeness of the contest was largely the result of the candidacy of George Wallace, which attracted many conservative Republican voters. Standing as an independent, Wallace gained almost 10 million votes. In a campaign against big business and government bureaucracy he drew strong support from northern blue-collar workers, and in Deep South states like Louisiana, Mississippi and Alabama. Wallace was renowned as the staunch segregationist Governor of Alabama during the mid-1960s; his appeal was a sign of white hostility to further action on black civil rights. For a time there appeared to be a serious possibility that another strong Wallace campaign in 1972 might prevent Nixon's re-election to the White House. Pre-empting this challenge, the Nixon administration adopted a 'southern strategy' designed to appeal to Wallace supporters.

Tough new measures on law and order were introduced. In the District of Columbia, perceived as having a large black criminal population, policies of no bail and preventative detention were implemented. Nationally, FBI Director J. Edgar Hoover used operation COINTELPRO to stifle opposition to the Nixon administration. Introduced in 1967 under President Johnson, COINTELPRO was a covert FBI campaign to discredit and sabotage the efforts of suspected subversives, who were seen as posing a threat to the internal security of the United States. In reality it was used against a wide range of groups and individuals, including Martin Luther King and the SCLC. COINTELPRO operations reached a peak in the Nixon years and were used as part of a wider policy of official persecution of Black Power groups and civil rights leaders. The SNCC was the subject of extensive FBI surveillance, and on 16 October 1971 Rap Brown was wounded in a shoot-out with police. In March 1973 Brown was convicted of armed robbery and assault and sentenced to five to ten years' imprisonment. In 1972 the 'Wilmington Ten', a group of civil rights protesters led by Reverend Benjamin Chavis, were arrested and charged with arson in North Carolina. The trial jury included three known members of the Ku Klux Klan, and the FBI bribed witnesses to testify against the defendants. The ten protesters were collectively sentenced to 282 years in jail.

The severest repression was directed against the Black Panthers, which was effectively destroyed as an organization by police and FBI actions between 1967 and 1969. In 1969 alone, 27 Panther members were shot dead by police and another 750 arrested. By 1970 most of the national leadership of the Panthers was either killed, imprisoned, or forced into exile overseas, as in the case of Eldridge Cleaver, who fled to Algeria in 1968 to avoid being jailed for alleged parole violations. George Jackson, a Panther activist, had in 1960, at the age of 18, been jailed for 'one year to life' for stealing $70 from a store. In 1971 he was shot dead by prison guards whilst trying to escape. The resulting public controversy that surrounded the incident was made worse by suspicions that the prison authorities had colluded in encouraging the escape attempt. Jackson's death sparked off a wave of national protests and was the catalyst for a major prison disorder in Attica, New York, where inmates took control of the penal institution for several days. In keeping with his tough law-and-order image, Nixon authorized the Governor of New York, Nelson Rockefeller, to storm the prison with National Guardsmen. Twenty-nine prisoners and ten prison guards were killed in the assault.

On specific issues of black civil rights the philosophy of the Nixon administration was one of 'benign neglect'. This resulted in frequent conflict with the Supreme Court, led by a new Chief Justice, Warren Burger, after the retirement of Earl Warren in 1969. In *Alexander* v. *Holmes County* (1969), the Burger Court ordered the immediate desegregation of public schools on the grounds that the 1955 'with all deliberate speed' ruling in the *Brown* case could no longer be used to justify further delay. From 1969 to 1974 the proportion of black children attending segregated schools dropped from 68 per cent to just 8 per cent.

In *Swann* v. *Charlotte Mecklenberg Board of Education* (1971), the court moved to resolve the problem of *de facto* school segregation that resulted from differing white and black residential patterns. The court approved plans requiring white children from suburban schools to be bused into largely black inner-city schools, whilst black ghetto pupils were bused out to schools in the suburbs. The 'busing' issue emerged as a major controversy in the early 1970s. Local white protest groups were formed to resist the imposition of busing, such as the 1974 'Restore Our Alienated Rights' (ROAR) campaign in Boston. Nixon publicly aligned himself with protesting white parents and refused to take any active measures to enforce the introduction of busing programmes. Retirements from the Burger Court enabled Nixon to secure the appointment of new conservative Supreme Court justices Harry Blackmun, Lewis Powell and William Rehnquist. Under their influence the court qualified its support for busing in the case of *Millican* v. *Bradley* (1974). Republican President Gerald Ford, 1974–7, who succeeded Nixon after the latter's resignation from office in the wake of the Watergate scandal, continued the same policy of non-intervention and spoke out in support of the ROAR campaign.

Taken as a whole the neglect of black civil rights was anything but benign in the Nixon and Ford years. The one exception to this was the introduction of 'affirmative action' or positive discrimination employment programmes. Under the 1969 Philadelphia Plan the Nixon administration required companies with contracts from the federal government to increase their proportion of workers from ethnic minority groups to 26 per cent within four years. In *Giggs* v. *Duke Power Company* (1971), the Supreme Court upheld the constitutionality of affirmative action. By 1972 some 300,000 businesses were bound by the new quotas.

Nixon's support for affirmative action was inconsistent with his general racial and economic conservatism. It was, however, in keeping with his wish to promote black capitalism. Moreover, the acute social and economic problems suffered by many African Americans made it difficult to avoid at least some action on their behalf. Partly for this reason, federal expenditure on social security and welfare payments doubled between January 1969 and August 1974. In 1975 federal expenditure on food stamps was $5,000 million, compared to only $36 million a year in the mid-1960s. Affirmative action also had the advantage of dividing Nixon's political opponents in the Democratic Party. Since the 1930s national electoral support for the Democratic Party had been built on a coalition of liberals, working-class whites, and ethnic-minority groups. Affirmative action appeared to promote greater job opportunities for African Americans at the expense of white workers. In responding to this initiative national Democratic Party leaders were thus placed in a position where it was almost impossible to avoid alienating at least one key group of electoral supporters. This basic dilemma persisted into the 1980s and the 1990s.

# CHAPTER FIVE

# Winter in America

## 1977 to the millennium

In the 1980s and the 1990s African Americans lived in interesting times. Many racial problems continued to be unresolved, and even worsened, yet there were also some advances. In political terms blacks achieved electoral success unknown since the 1860s and the 1870s. In 1971 black congressmen of all political persuasions founded the Congressional Black Caucus (CBC), which became an important pressure group campaigning on racial issues. In 1994 there were over 40 black congressmen, including Carol Mosely Brown, an Illinois Democrat who in 1992 became the first African American woman to be elected to the US Senate. Success at national level was repeated at the grassroots with the election of numerous blacks to local political office. Most spectacular was the election of black mayors in leading cities throughout the United States. These included Harold Washington in Chicago, David Dinkins in New York City, Thomas Bradley in Los Angeles, Wilson Good in Philadelphia, Andrew Young in Atlanta and Marion Barry in Washington, DC.

Despite these high-profile gains, in 1994 African Americans comprised some 12.5 per cent of the US population but made up only 2 per cent of elected and appointed officials. Moreover, electoral success was often short-lived. Carol Mosely Brown failed to secure re-election in 1998. In 1987 Harold Washington was re-elected as Mayor of Chicago, but died shortly afterwards. He was succeeded by the white Democrat Richard M. Daley, son of former Mayor Richard J. Daley. In New York City David Dinkins was defeated in 1993 by Republican Rudolf Guiliani. In 1990 Marion Barry was arrested by the FBI and convicted and jailed for drug offences.

Portraying himself as the victim of official persecution, Barry was, however, re-elected as mayor in 1994 by Washington, DC's majority black electorate.

Ironically, the best-known and most influential black political figure of the 1980s and 1990s, Jesse Jackson, held no elected office at all. Born the son of a sharecropper in Greensville, South Carolina in 1941, Jackson first attended the University of Illinois, 1959–60, before graduating with a BA in sociology and economics from the all-black North Carolina Agricultural and Technical State University in 1964. He was actively involved in the Greensboro sit-in movement and subsequently became a civil rights activist with the SCLC. From 1964 to 1966 he studied for the ministry at the Chicago Theological Seminary, but left before graduation to take up full-time employment with the SCLC.

His knowledge of the Windy City led to Jackson's becoming a leading local organizer during Martin Luther King's 1966 Chicago campaign. Jackson was given responsibility for Operation Bread-basket, which sought to achieve better employment opportunities for blacks in the city. By 1967 Jackson had helped to secure some 2,200 new jobs for African Americans in white-owned Chicago businesses. This success led to a growing recognition of Jackson's ability.

At the same time King had misgivings about Jackson's leadership potential. He believed that Jackson was too conservative in his philosophy, looking to private-sector solutions for poverty and racism rather than recognizing the need for public-sector action and a fundamental restructuring of US society. King also felt that Jackson sometimes put his own personal ambition before the good of the civil rights movement as a whole. This latter suspicion appeared to be borne out following the assassination of Martin Luther King on 4 April 1968. When King was shot, Jackson was standing next to him. The same evening he made a controversial appearance on network television giving a detailed account of how he had cradled the head of the dying SCLC leader.

In May 1968 Jackson was given the symbolic role of Mayor of Resurrection City, the centrepiece of the SCLC's Poor People's campaign in Washington, DC. The failure of the campaign was a setback for Jackson. He also had strong personal differences with the SCLC's new president, Ralph Abernathy. In 1971 these tensions led to Jackson's suspension and later resignation from the SCLC.

During the 1970s Jackson's independent leadership status was confirmed by the establishment of his own organization, People United to Save Humanity (PUSH), later changed to the more modest People United to Serve Humanity. PUSH sought to replicate the success of Operation Breadbasket on a nationwide scale. Prominent national and international companies were targeted for customer boycotts and negative media campaigns unless they agreed to create more job opportunities for blacks. In August 1981 Coca-Cola signed an agreement with PUSH to invest $14 million in minority vendors and pledged to raise the proportion of blacks in its workforce from 5 per cent to 12.5 per cent. Similar agreements were reached with Burger King and Kentucky Fried Chicken. In 1982 PUSH negotiated a deal with the Seven Up Corporation to invest $61 million in black businesses. PUSH itself purchased shares in Ford, General Motors and Chrysler. In an offshoot initiative launched in 1975, Project PUSH Excel sought to raise educational standards and achievements among black school children.

In 1983–4 the high-profile success of PUSH campaigns encouraged Jackson to stand as a candidate for President of the United States. Seeking the nomination of the Democratic Party, the Jackson campaign was in part a reaction to the extreme conservatism of the administration of Republican President Ronald Reagan, 1981–9. A low black voter turn-out was a significant factor in the election of Reagan in 1980. Jackson's candidacy sought to increase the level of black voter participation and to promote a left of centre political agenda as an alternative to the Reagan programme.

The Jackson campaign was initially repudiated by mainstream African American leaders, including John Jacob, National Director of the NUL, Benjamin Hooks, Executive Secretary of the NAACP, and Martin Luther King's widow, Coretta Scott King. In an echo of the earlier views of Martin Luther King it was argued that the Jackson candidacy was an act of self-promotion that offered little prospect of any tangible gain for African Americans. Instead, Jackson would divide the Democratic Party and produce a conservative white electoral backlash. Similar criticisms were put forward by the black academic commentator Adolph Reed in a 1986 study, *The Jesse Jackson Phenomenon: The Crisis of Purpose in Afro-American Politics*. Reed argued that the Jackson campaign was a meaningless media event. Moreover, Jackson represented an outdated and hierarchical style of church leadership that dated back to the civil rights movement of the 1950s and 1960s. In the 1980s this was no longer relevant because church leaders had been replaced by a new generation of elected black politicians.

Jackson's response to his critics was to deny that he was just a black civil rights leader. Instead, he sought to appeal to a broad constituency of support, a 'rainbow coalition' of ethnic-minority groups and the poor and dispossessed of all races. During his election bid he not only spoke out on racial and social issues but also put forward radical proposals on foreign policy and defence. These included calls for the removal of cruise missiles from Europe, an end to US intervention in Central America, the restoration of diplomatic relations with Cuba, and the creation of a Palestinian homeland in the Middle East.

At the July 1984 Democratic Party National Convention in San Francisco, Jackson predictably fell well short of the level of support needed to win the party's presidential nomination. Nonetheless, he had the backing of 465 delegates, compared to 1,200 delegates for Gary Hart and 2,191 delegates for the party's chosen presidential candidate, Walter Mondale.

In 1988 Jackson used his base of support to launch a second presidential campaign. The heavy defeat of Mondale by Reagan in the 1984 election helped Jackson to portray himself as the only genuine alternative challenger in 1988. Moving beyond the boundaries of race, he again put forward policy proposals on a broad range of issues, and he was able to command support from all sections of the Democratic Party. In the 1987–8 primary campaign Jackson won the backing of over 7 million voters and won primaries in 13 states. This included the Wisconsin primary of 3 April 1988, a state in which blacks made up less than 4 per cent of the population. At the July 1988 Democratic Party National Convention in Atlanta Jackson had the support of 1,200 delegates and was runner-up to the party's chosen presidential candidate, Michael Dukakis, with 2,800 delegates.

His two election campaigns in the 1980s brought Jackson national and international recognition. They also established him as the most important African American spokesperson within the Democratic Party. At both the 1984 and the 1988 Democratic Party National Conventions he gave powerful and emotive speeches to party delegates that were covered live on prime-time network television. He was, however, unable to convert this new-found status to tangible political gains. Rejected as a vice-presidential running mate by both Mondale and Dukakis, he also had little impact on the policy platform of either candidate. Despite their unexpected success the two Jackson campaigns ultimately failed to lay to rest the charges of empty symbolism that were levelled against them.

Moreover, Jackson's status as a political figure was tarnished by his links with NOI leader Louis Farrakhan. A close supporter of Jackson, in April 1984 Farrakhan made controversial public comments that were seen as anti-semitic, calling Judaism a 'gutter religion'. In a private conversation Jackson himself was reported as referring to New York City, with its large Jewish community, as 'Hymie town'. Even though he severed links with the NOI, Jackson's 1984 election bid was seriously damaged. Lingering public concern over the incident continued to be a harmful, albeit less significant, issue during his 1988 campaign.

During the 1980s and 1990s gains made by African Americans were not confined to political life. Significant numbers of blacks achieved advances in employment in the professions and at managerial level. The 1990 US census showed that over 9 million of the 31 million African Americans in the United States lived in households with a total annual income of at least $35,000, the conventional benchmark of middle-class status. By the mid-1990s one in six black households had incomes in excess of $50,000 a year.

In a widely publicized work, *The Declining Significance of Race* (1978), the black sociologist William Julius Wilson argued that the emergence of this new black middle class marked a turning point in US race relations. The main source of division in American society at the end of the twentieth century was no longer race but class, the divide between the rich and the poor. This claim has been extensively criticized. Whatever the economic gains of some African Americans, race relations clearly remained a deeply controversial issue throughout the 1980s and 1990s. Moreover, the new black economic elite comprised only a small proportion of African American families. During the 1990s 31 per cent of all African American families were officially classified as poor, compared to only 10 per cent of white families. Black Americans were over twice as likely to be unemployed as whites, and black youth unemployment in the major urban ghettos regularly exceeded 50 per cent.

These depressing statistics highlighted the failure of successive presidential administrations to improve living conditions for the majority of African Americans. The presidency of Jimmy Carter, 1977–81, initially appeared to offer new hope for blacks. A southern liberal Democrat, Carter was sympathetic to civil rights campaigners. He appointed a number of blacks to important political posts, including Andrew Young as US ambassador to the United Nations, Patricia Harris as Secretary of Housing and Urban Development, Eleanor Holmes Norton as Head of the Equal Employment Opportunities Commission and Wade McCree as Solicitor General. In July 1979, when Andrew Young was forced to resign because of his support for the Palestine Liberation Organization (PLO), Carter chose another African American, Donald McHenry, to succeed him.

In the diplomatic service Carter appointed 14 black ambassadors. These served not only in the Third World posts traditionally set aside for ethnic-minority appointees, but also in embassies in Europe. In the judiciary Carter appointed more blacks, Hispanics and women as federal judges than all previous Presidents. He made Louis Martin, an African American, a special adviser on civil rights and met regularly with black leaders during his term of office.

Despite such positive actions, as early as August 1977 Carter was publicly accused of the 'callous neglect' of African Americans by leading black spokesmen. These included Jesse Jackson, Bayard Rustin, Vernon Jordan, Executive Director of the NUL, and Benjamin Hooks, who succeeded Roy Wilkins as Executive Secretary of the NAACP in 1977. In part this criticism resulted from the fact that civil rights leaders had had unrealistically high expectations of the Carter presidency. Carter's election was seen as marking a return to the golden era of the Johnson years.

In the changing climate of the 1970s this was not possible. There was no longer strong political support for civil rights initiatives. The US economy was in recession, suffering from 'stagflation', an unpleasant combination of high inflation and rising unemployment. Black workers, many of whom were unskilled, were particularly badly hit by job losses. At the same time declining tax revenues meant that less money was available for federal social and welfare programmes. In May 1980 a major race riot in the African American quarter of Miami, Florida, symbolized the inability of the Carter administration to deal with the problems of poor black ghetto dwellers. The worst urban disorder since the 1960s, the riot resulted in 18 deaths, 400 people injured, 1,250 arrests and $100 million in property damage.

The Supreme Court under Carter, with its majority of Republican appointees, seemed unsure of its philosophy on civil rights. In *Regents of the University of California* v. *Bakke* (1978), Allan Bakke, a white student, claimed that he had been unfairly denied admission to the University because of its policy of positive discrimination in favour of black students. The court held that this affirmative action programme was unconstitutional. At the same time it ruled that race could still be a 'determining factor' in University admissions procedures. In *Fullilove* v. *Klutznick* (1980), the court upheld a 1977 federal law that set aside a 10 per cent quota for minority businesses in public-works contracts. The judges also acknowledged the need to counter *de facto* as well as *de jure* discrimination, even if this might adversely affect the interests of innocent third parties.

The legitimacy of affirmative action programmes and racial quotas became a major issue under the two administrations of Republican President Ronald Reagan, 1981–9. A right-wing conservative, Reagan claimed that the advances made in race relations since the 1960s meant that positive discrimination in favour of ethnic minorities was no longer necessary. On the contrary, such measures unfairly discriminated against whites. William Bradford Reynolds, Assistant Attorney General for Civil Rights in the Justice Department, became a leading adviser in the Reagan administration. Reynolds tried to remove or weaken affirmative action programmes, championing 'individual opportunity over group entitlements'. The Carter administration had required businesses with 50 or more workers in receipt of federal government contracts of over $50,000 to submit written affirmative action programmes. Under Reagan the threshold was raised to firms with 250 or more employees and only applied to federal contracts in excess of $1,000,000.

There were severe cutbacks in the level of federal expenditure on social and welfare programmes during the Reagan years. Conservative Republicans claimed that such measures interfered with natural market forces, imposed an unfair burden on taxpayers, and created a culture of dependency. In 1988 the Family Support Act compelled welfare recipients to do community-service work or participate in government-approved training programmes. Enduring poverty in African American communities meant that blacks as a group were particularly hard hit by such measures.

In public, administration spokespersons denied any allegations of racism. At the same time, campaign speeches by Reagan to white audiences portrayed ethnic minorities as 'quota kings' and 'welfare queens' who gained unfair advantages from federal handouts. Moreover, Reagan opposed the plan to make Martin Luther King's birthday on 20 January into a public holiday. He only gave his reluctant consent, in 1983, when it became clear that there was strong congressional support for this measure. The same year Reagan publicly supported the right of the conservative Bob Jones University in Greensville, South Carolina, to enjoy tax-exempt status. The fact that Bob Jones routinely segregated its white and black students and banned interracial dating led to the Supreme Court ruling against the University. Predictably, only one African American, Samuel R. Pierce, Secretary of Housing and Urban Development, was appointed to cabinet rank in the Reagan years.

Republican President George Bush, 1989–93, pledged that his administration would bring about a 'kinder, gentler America'. In practice Bush, who had served as Vice-President under Reagan, continued with many of the policies of his predecessor. During the 1988 election Bush's campaign manager, Lee Atwater, pursued a controversial strategy of 'negative campaigning'. This sought to portray Bush's Democratic opponent, Michael Dukakis, as a weak liberal who was soft on crime and welfare spongers. A centrepiece of this exercise was the case of Willie Horton, an African American in prison for murder in Massachusetts, the state in which Dukakis was Governor. Massachusetts, like many other states, had a furlough rehabilitation programme that allowed long-term inmates occasional brief periods of release from jail. On one such furlough, in April 1987, Horton had kidnapped and raped a white woman. Television advertising and public statements by the Bush camp repeatedly cited the Horton case as proof of the unfitness of Dukakis for presidential office.

Once in the White House, Bush continued to exploit racial divisions and fears about crime for political advantage. During 1990–1 he repeatedly vetoed a minor congressional civil rights bill as a 'quota' measure before finally giving his consent for it to become law. An administration-backed crime Act provided an additional $1.4 million in funds for federal judges and prosecutors, but only an extra $150,000 for public defence lawyers.

The increasingly *laissez-faire* philosophy of the Supreme Court in the 1980s was reinforced by the elevation of Nixon appointee William Rehnquist to Chief Justice in 1986. New conservative judges were also appointed to the court. These included Antonin Scalia and Anthony Kennedy under Reagan and David Souter and Clarence Thomas under Bush.

Bush's 1991 nomination of Clarence Thomas created particular controversy. Thomas, although African American, was a conservative Republican who opposed the continuation of affirmative action programmes. This was despite the fact that he had personally benefited from positive discrimination measures during his own career. At his confirmation hearings, before the US Senate, Thomas was accused of sexual harassment by a black female former employee, Anita Hill. Civil rights leaders and advocates of women's rights united in public opposition to Thomas. Televised appearances by Thomas and other witnesses before the Senate led to embarrassing, damaging disclosures about his private life and sexual mores. Thomas defended himself by suggesting that his detractors were motivated by racial bigotry, and that he was the victim of a 'high-tech lynching'. In making such claims he ironically appeared to repudiate his generally held view that racism was largely a problem of the past and that African Americans no longer needed any special treatment or privileges.

The election of William Jefferson Clinton in November 1992 ended 12 years of Republican occupation of the White House. Clinton presented himself as a 'new Democrat', sensitive to the needs of the poor and ethnic minorities, but also committed to low taxation and moderation in government spending. Caring, but responsive to the feelings of middle-class Americans, Clinton's voter-centred pragmatism was highlighted in his 1991–2 election campaign. In January 1992, as Governor of Arkansas, he authorized the execution of a brain-damaged African American murderer, Rickey Ray Rector. He ignored pleas for clemency by Jesse Jackson; his support for the death penalty prevented any re-emergence of the Willie Horton factor.

On 13 June 1992 Clinton made use of Jesse Jackson himself for electoral advantage. Attending a meeting of the Rainbow Coalition organization in Washington, DC, Clinton publicly rebuked Jackson over the presence of 'Sister Souljah', a controversial black Rap artist. After race riots in Los Angeles in April 1992 Souljah had asked 'If black people kill black people every day, why not have a week and kill white people?' Clinton's symbolic reprimand neutralized fears among white blue-collar workers that he was too dependent on Jackson's advice and support.

Inaugurated as President in January 1993, Clinton lived up to his campaign promise to form an administration that reflected all America. He appointed numerous women and ethnic-minority leaders to government posts, including African Americans Ron Brown as Commerce Secretary and Hazel O'Leary as Energy Secretary. Fourteen out of 48 federal judges appointed by Clinton during his first year of office were African Americans.

At the same time, Clinton was influenced by the hostility of white voters to affirmative action programmes and racial quotas. In 1993 he nominated Lani Guinier, an African American woman, as Assistant Attorney General for Civil Rights. He later withdrew his support for her after press reports that portrayed Guinier as a 'quota queen' who championed affirmative action. Another African American woman, Jocelyn Elders, was appointed as Surgeon General of the United States but forced to resign because of conservative opposition to her liberal views on contraception and sex education. Henry Foster, an African American selected by Clinton to replace Elders, was forced to withdraw after a Republican campaign against him because he had previously carried out abortions.

In his policies Clinton was constantly forced to take account of conservative public opinion, Republican opposition in Congress, and the perceived liberal excesses of previous Democratic administrations. In August 1994 the omnibus Crime Control Act introduced the death penalty for 58 new offences and a 'three strikes and you are out' policy of mandatory life sentences for repeat offenders. The Act was supported both by Clinton himself and by 'law-and-order' Republicans. The same year, Republican opposition in Congress led to the failure of Clinton's major initiative on health-care reform, which had sought to provide health insurance for all, subsidized by the federal government. The defeat of the proposal was a particular blow to African Americans, many of whom were too poor to afford private medical care. During the 1990s over 20 per cent of African Americans had no health insurance cover.

The mid-term congressional elections of November 1994 further weakened the position of the Clinton administration. Campaigning on a far right-wing manifesto, the 'Contract with America', Republican candidates made sweeping gains to achieve control of both houses of Congress. In 1995–6 Clinton was able to recover some lost political ground by presenting himself as a moderate in the face of radical Republican proposals for tax reductions and drastic cuts in welfare spending. This image helped the President to secure re-election in November 1996. Nonetheless, the Republicans retained control of both the US Senate and the House of Representatives, a position that they maintained after the congressional elections of November 1998.

Although Clinton was able to veto some Republican congressional initiatives, he also had to make concessions. The most far-reaching of these was the passage of the Personal Responsibility and Work Opportunity Act in August 1996. This Act largely dismantled the 1935 Social Security Act, which had been introduced by Roosevelt as a part of the New Deal. The 1996 legislation limited welfare claimants to a maximum of three years of benefit throughout their life. The responsibility for welfare payments was shifted from the federal government to individual state governments. States were given block federal grants to provide Temporary Assistance to Needy Families (TANF). The level of benefit payments made to claimants was left up to each state to resolve, as was the problem of insufficient funds being available in the event of a severe recession. Proportionately more reliant on welfare provision than whites, African Americans were among the groups most adversely affected by these changes.

The Supreme Court under Clinton continued to qualify its support for affirmative action programmes. This was despite the successful nomination of two new justices, Ruth Bader Ginsberg and Stephen Breyer, by the President, both of whom were comparatively liberal in their outlook. In *Adarond Construction* v. *Pera* (1995), the court ruled that in future, affirmative action programmes should be subject to 'strict scrutiny' and used only in specific instances to counter clear cases of discrimination. Encouraged by this decision, in 1996 voters in California approved the passage of Proposition 209, an initiative that banned race- and gender-based affirmative action programmes in the Golden State.

African American leaders, like the Democratic Party, struggled to adapt to the new conservatism of the 1980s and 1990s. A minority of black spokespersons responded by themselves embracing right-wing values. These included Supreme Court judge Clarence Thomas, Republican congressmen Gary Franks and J. C. Watts, the academic economist Thomas Sowell and sociologist William Julius Wilson.

Snubbed by Clinton in 1992, Jesse Jackson found it difficult to maintain the political momentum that he had achieved in the 1980s.

The growing number of African Americans elected as congressmen and city mayors meant that he was no longer seen as the only black spokesperson of national importance within the Democratic Party. He declined to stand again for the presidency in 1992 and 1996, and in March 1999 announced that he would not be a candidate in the year 2000. Although his son, Jesse Jackson Jr, was elected to the US House of Representatives in December 1995, Jackson himself was no longer a serious candidate for political office.

Jackson sought fulfilment in other ways. His merged Rainbow-PUSH organization continued to campaign for better employment opportunities for blacks. Working in alliance with the NAACP, he helped to secure an agreement from the Texaco Corporation to improve its hiring practices for minority employees. In March and April 1999 he launched a new black voter registration campaign and targeted Wall Street and Silicon Valley to improve the representation of minorities on company boards. Rainbow-PUSH purchased small amounts of stock in over 200 major companies to gain the right to attend and ask questions at shareholder meetings.

Domestically, Jackson retained his high public profile as a regular participant in civil rights rallies and demonstrations, and through his television talk show, *Both Sides with Jesse Jackson*, on CNN. Internationally, Jackson served as a special diplomatic envoy for the Clinton administration. During 1994 he was a US observer at South Africa's first multi-racial elections, and on 1 May 1999 he successfully met with President Milosevic to secure the release of three US servicemen captured during NATO bombings of Serbia.

In addition to developments in the national climate of race relations, the NAACP suffered the problem of internal division. During 1993 Benjamin Chavis narrowly defeated Jesse Jackson to be appointed Executive Director of the NAACP. A veteran civil rights campaigner who had suffered imprisonment during the 1970s, Chavis introduced a number of controversial new initiatives. Despite falling NAACP revenue in April 1994, at a cost of $125,000 he sent a 14-person delegation to observe Nelson Mandela's election campaign in South Africa. In July he pushed through a $75,000 proposal to establish a permanent NAACP office in South Africa.

At home Chavis sought to make the NAACP more attractive to younger African Americans by developing links with black nationalists and militants. In June 1994 he invited Louis Farrakhan, head of the Nation of Islam, to attend a two-day National African

American Leadership Summit. Farrakhan's outspoken views were unacceptable to many NAACP members. His belief in racial separatism was seen as incompatible with the NAACP's commitment to integration.

Further doubts about Chavis's leadership were raised by revelations that he had used over $300,000 in NAACP funds to settle a sexual harassment lawsuit brought against him by a former employee. Faced with a damaging public scandal, in August 1994 the NAACP Board sacked Chavis and installed field secretary Earl Shinhoster as a caretaker leader. Continuing financial problems left the NAACP $3.2 million in debt by early 1996. The image of the organization was further damaged by the dismissal of NAACP Board member Hazel Dukes in December 1997 for financial impropriety and unethical conduct.

The NAACP began to overcome its problems in the late 1990s. In February 1996 Kweisi Mfume was appointed as the NAACP's new Executive Director. A five-term congressman from Maryland and head of the Congressional Black Caucus, he brought considerable experience to the post. Within nine months the NAACP was back on a sound financial footing and its debts were expunged. In November 1996 the Texaco settlement marked another breakthrough. In February 1998 the veteran civil rights campaigner, politician, broadcaster and academic Julian Bond became NAACP Board Chairman. Bond was a widely respected national figure, and former friend and colleague of Martin Luther King; his appointment confirmed the NAACP's reformed image.

During the 1990s Louis Farrakhan emerged as the best-known and most controversial African American leader. Born as Louis Walcott in New York City in 1933, Farrakhan trained as a school teacher before becoming a Boston cabaret musician in 1954. After coming into contact with Malcolm X and Elijah Muhammed he gave up his show-business career in 1955, joined the NOI and adopted the name Louis X. At the end of 1963 he replaced Malcolm X as the National Minister of the Nation, becoming Muhammed's second in command. In February 1965 he was suspected of plotting the assassination of Malcolm X, but no charges were ever brought. When Elijah Muhammed died in 1975 his son Wallace Muhammed sought to convert the NOI to orthodox Islamic practices and beliefs. He changed the name of the organization to the World Community of Islam. Leading a breakaway faction, in 1978 Louis X, now known as Louis Farrakhan, revived the former Nation according to the teachings of Elijah Muhammed.

During 1983–4 Farrakhan attracted national media attention as a close supporter of Jesse Jackson's presidential campaign. In April 1984, however, the public controversy surrounding his perceived anti-semitism, and his subsequent break with Jackson, damaged Farrakhan's position as a race leader. He remained largely marginalized for the rest of the 1980s.

Between 1993 and 1995 Farrakhan re-emerged to achieve important mainstream recognition. During September 1993, along with a range of other organizations, the NOI entered into a 'Sacred Covenant' with the CBC to promote black self-help. In June 1994 Farrakhan was invited to the NAACP's National African American Leadership Summit. Most important of all, in early 1995 he managed to mend a 30-year rift with the family of Malcolm X. Betty Shabbaz, Malcolm X's widow, had consistently claimed that Farrakhan had been implicated in her husband's death. In January 1995 Qubilah Shabbaz, Malcolm X's daughter, was charged by the FBI with plotting to murder Farrakhan. The NOI leader came to her defence, supporting her claims that she was a victim of FBI entrapment. The charges were eventually dropped and Farrakhan was publicly reconciled with Qubilah and her family.

Farrakhan's growing status was demonstrated in the Million Man March on 16 October 1995. A major one-off rally in Washington, DC the march, organized by Farrakhan, was intended as a 'Day of Atonement' by black men for their failure to take responsibility for their partners and families. The event was widely criticized in advance by national white and black leaders and also black women who were officially excluded from the event. Despite this the march attracted a number of prominent speakers, including Jesse Jackson and members of the CBC. At least 400,000 African American men, and possibly as many as 1,000,000, took part in the rally. This was well in excess of the 250,000 whites and blacks who attended the celebrated March on Washington in 1963.

On 16 October 1996, the first anniversary of the Million Man March, Farrakhan was the leading organizer and speaker at a 'World Day of Atonement' in another major rally held in New York City. In October 1997 over 100 cities commemorated the second anniversary of the 'Day of Atonement', reflecting Farrakhan's stated hope that the occasion would be turned into an annual religious festival. Women's groups organized a Million Woman March in Philadelphia. In September 1998 the NOI, in conjunction with the NAACP, the Rainbow-PUSH coalition and other groups, organized a week-long Million Youth Movement in Atlanta.

Despite his considerable influence in African American communities, Farrakhan was condemned frequently by leading politicians and civil rights leaders. Allegations of anti-semitism and racism persisted. Farrakhan himself often made seemingly anti-semitic comments and, in October 1991, the NOI's Historical Research Department published *The Secret Relationship between Blacks and Jews*. This work accused Jews of 'monumental culpability' in slavery and the slave trade. In November 1993 Khalid Muhammed, NOI National Spokesman, gave a provocative address to black students at Kean College, New Jersey, calling Jews the 'bloodsuckers of the black nation'. The speech also denounced whites, Catholics and homosexuals. In the public furore that resulted, Muhammed was temporarily suspended from his position by Farrakhan but continued to be a prominent figure within the NOI.

Domestically, the NOI had periodic links with white supremacist organizations, including the Ku Klux Klan, White Aryan Resistance and the American Nazi Party. Internationally, Farrakhan maintained contacts with a number of despotic, undemocratic regimes. In February 1996 he embarked on an 18-nation overseas tour, meeting with, amongst others, the military regime of Nigeria, Libyan leader Colonel Gaddafi, and Saddam Hussein of Iraq. The trip was labelled a 'thugfest' by White House spokesman Mike McCurry.

Farrakhan was also accused of homophobia and sexism. The NOI's religious beliefs stressed that homosexuality was morally wrong, that Muslim women should submit to the will of their husbands, and that the principal role of women in society was as wives and mothers. During 1992 Farrakhan supported black World Heavyweight Boxing Champion Mike Tyson when the latter was accused of raping black beauty queen Desiree Washington. Public remarks by Farrakhan appeared to suggest that he believed that Washington had brought the rape on herself by admitting Tyson into her hotel room.

Farrakhan's appeal to African Americans, particularly young black men in the ghettos, derived from a variety of sources. He encouraged blacks to take pride in their racial identity. Rap artists such as Public Enemy and Ice Cube promoted Farrakhan's teachings

in their lyrics. The NOI worked to achieve black self-help and economic empowerment in the inner cities. In 1981, People Organized
and Working for Economic Rebirth (POWER), an NOI initiative,
sought to set up new black businesses. During 1990 Farrakhan
embarked on a nationwide 'Stop the Killing' tour to reduce black-
on-black ghetto violence. From 1988 to 1995 NOI security patrols
in Washington, DC, New York City, Chicago, Los Angeles and
other leading US cities sought to keep drugs and crime out of black
neighbourhoods.

Despite such initiatives, Farrakhan, like other black leaders of
the 1990s, failed to offer any long-term solutions to the problems
faced by African Americans. The Million Man March of 1995 did not
result in any lasting momentum or permanent organization for
change. Actual membership of the NOI remained small and the sect
experienced growing financial problems. These worsened in August
1996 when the Clinton administration refused to allow Farrakhan
to accept a $250,000 'Human Rights Award' and a $1,000 million
gift from Colonel Gaddafi of Libya.

Relations between African Americans and the US legal system in
the 1980s and 1990s were a continuing source of tension. Between
1983 and 1996 the total US prison population more than doubled,
from 650,000 to 1.6 million. African Americans, although only 12.5
per cent of the US population, regularly made up 45–50 per cent of
prison inmates. In 1995–6 nearly one-third of all African American
men in their twenties were either in prison, on probation, on parole
or awaiting trial. In any given year during the 1990s more than 1 in
20 of all African American males in their twenties were murder
victims. These disturbing statistics were partly the consequence of
high levels of social and economic deprivation in many African
American communities, particularly in the major urban ghettos. The
persistence of institutionalized racism within city, state and federal
law-enforcement agencies was another major problem. Many black
Americans had little faith in the capacity of the legal system to deliver
fair and impartial justice where racial issues were involved. This was
reflected in a number of high-profile court cases.

In November 1987 Tawana Brawley, a 15-year-old African
American girl in New York City, was reported as missing by her
family. She was found tied up in a garbage bag smeared with dog
faeces and with racist phrases scrawled on her body. Taken to
hospital for treatment, she claimed to have been gang-raped by six

white law-enforcement officers. These included Assistant District Attorney Steven Pagones. The case became a subject of national media attention and Brawley received support from prominent African Americans such as the actor Bill Cosby, Mike Tyson and the New York clergyman and civil rights activist Al Sharpton. In October 1988 an investigating grand jury dismissed Brawley's claims as a hoax, although many important questions remained unanswered. Sharpton, along with Brawley's legal advisers, Alton Maddox and C. Vernon Mason, continued to denounce Pagones as a rapist on radio and television. In July 1998 Pagones was awarded damages of $345,000 against Sharpton, Maddox and Mason in a defamation lawsuit. Brawley herself was ordered to pay Pagones a further $185,000.

In March 1991 Rodney King, a black motorist in Los Angeles, was stopped and badly beaten by members of the Los Angeles Police Department (LAPD). The incident was recorded on video by a chance onlooker. Despite this evidence, in April 1992 the police officers involved were acquitted of all criminal charges by a white California jury. The verdicts sparked off three days of race riots in Los Angeles. Fifty-two people were killed, 2,285 injured, and 16,291 arrested. Twenty thousand police officers and national guardsmen were needed to restore order, and over $1,000 million was lost in property damage. Live footage of the rioting was relayed on network television by helicopter camera crews. Racial tensions were highlighted during the disorder as Korean shops and businesses were targeted by black looters. La Tasha Harlins, an African American girl, was shot in a confrontation with a Korean shopkeeper. The incident was recorded by television cameras, as was the beating of Reginald Denny, a white lorry driver seized from his cab by black rioters. Denny avoided an even worse fate after being rescued by other African Americans at the scene.

Three years later another legal case in California attracted even more national media attention. From January to October 1995 the former African American football star O. J. Simpson was put on trial in Los Angeles for the murder of his wife, Nicole Brown Simpson, and her friend Ronald Goldman. Both murder victims were white. Simpson had a record of domestic violence against Nicole Brown and the case against him was strong.

During the trial Simpson's defence lawyers, the 'dream team', which included African American Johnnie Cochran, claimed that

Simpson had been framed by the LAPD. Evidence was produced that appeared to prove that one of the lead detectives in the investigation, Mark Fuhrman, was a racist who had lied under oath on the witness stand. The jury, the majority of whom were non-white, found Simpson not guilty.

The whole trial was covered live on network television and polarized the nation along racial lines. A CNN/*Time Magazine* survey after the verdict revealed that 62 per cent of white Americans polled were convinced that Simpson was guilty, whist 21 per cent believed him innocent. In sharp contrast, 14 per cent of African Americans polled believed Simpson to be guilty and 66 per cent thought him not guilty. Fifty-one per cent of whites in the poll and 88 per cent of blacks agreed that the Simpson verdict had increased racial tensions in the United States. A civil prosecution, requiring a lower burden of proof, was later brought against Simpson by the Goldman and Brown families. This lawsuit was successful, and in February 1997 Simpson was ordered to pay damages of $35.5 million.

Relations between African Americans and police forces in California remained troubled in the second half of the 1990s. On 28 December 1998 Tyisha Miller, a 19-year-old African American woman, was shot 12 times and killed by police in Riverside, a community near Los Angeles. In May 1999 Johnnie Cochran, acting as an attorney for her bereaved family, initiated a civil lawsuit against police officers involved in the incident. They were alleged to have shouted racial abuse at the victim and to have engaged in joyful celebrations after the shooting.

In the spring and summer of 1999 the American Civil Liberties Union (ACLU), and African American spokespersons, such as Jesse Jackson and Al Sharpton, expressed concern at police harassment of blacks across the United States. Police forces in California, New Jersey, Ohio, Florida, Maryland and Connecticut were accused of engaging in racial profiling – the stopping and questioning of people from ethnic-minority backgrounds for no other reason than their skin colour. African American motorists complained of being stopped for the offence of 'driving while black'. In May 1999 the CBC began a national series of hearings on alleged police brutality.

On the East Coast the treatment of ethnic minorities by police forces in New York City was an issue of controversy throughout the 1990s. The Republican administration of Mayor Rudolf Guiliani, elected in 1993, was committed to improving law and order in the city. This resulted in new aggressive patrolling by the New York Police Department (NYPD) and a policy of 'zero tolerance' for any law violations. Public concern at these measures was heightened by evidence of racism within the NYPD.

In August 1997 Abner Louima, a Haitian immigrant, was arrested by police in Brooklyn. Held in custody, he was sexually assaulted with a toilet plunger, suffering internal injuries that required three hospital operations. In May and June 1999 two police officers, Charles Schwarz and Justin Volpe, were convicted of the attack. In August 1998 Michael Jones, a black teenager carrying a water pistol that resembled a submachine gun, was shot six times by NYPD officers.

On 4 February 1999 Amadou Diallo, a 22-year-old West African immigrant, was shot dead by four white police officers outside his home in the Bronx. Diallo, who had no criminal record, was hit by 19 bullets. In a wave of public demonstrations in the city that followed the killing, over 1,175 protesters were arrested, including Jesse Jackson, Al Sharpton, former New York City Mayor David Dinkins, Kweisi Mfume and actors Ossie Davis, Ruby Dee and Susan Sarandon. In counter-demonstrations 500 off-duty police officers rallied in support of their colleagues. The four officers involved in the shooting were indicted on charges of second-degree murder but acquitted by a mixed race jury in February 2000.

Densely populated and multi-racial, New York City was the site of a number of disturbing racially motivated crimes in the late 1980s and the 1990s. In the Howard Beach case of 20 December 1986 an African American, Michael Griffith, was killed in a motoring incident in the Queens district of the city. Griffith had run into the road whilst fleeing a mob of racist white youths. On 23 August 1989 Yusuf Hawkins, a 16-year-old black American, was shot and beaten to death by white racists in Bensonhurst, Brooklyn. In another incident the following year a white woman jogger was brutally gang-raped by African American assailants in Central Park. During August 1991 a race riot broke out in Crown Heights, Brooklyn after a 7-year-old black child was accidentally killed by a Hasidic Jewish motorist. In the disorder Yonkel Rosenbaum, a visiting Jewish student from Australia, was stabbed to death by black protesters. Lemrick Nelson, a member of the mob, was jailed for 19½ years for the killing in April 1998. In December 1993, an African American, Colin Ferguson, boarded a packed commuter train on Long Island

and indiscriminately shot and killed white passengers. Khalid Muhammed, of the NOI, publicly responded to the incident by claiming that he loved Ferguson and that God had said to him 'Catch the train, Colin, catch the train!'

In the nation as a whole the last quarter of the twentieth century saw a worrying increase in the number of racist and politically extremist organizations. At Greensboro, North Carolina, on 3 November 1979, five unarmed civil rights protesters were shot and killed by members of the Ku Klux Klan. Despite the incident's being recorded on film the six Klansmen brought to trial for the shootings were acquitted by a white jury on the grounds of self-defence.

From 1989 to 1991 David Duke, Imperial Wizard of the Ku Klux Klan from 1974 to 1979, served a partial term as a Republican member for New Orleans in the state legislature of Louisiana. In 1990 Duke contested a US Senate seat in Louisiana, and the following year stood as a candidate for state Governor. Although unsuccessful on each occasion, his two campaigns attracted the support of 44 per cent and 39 per cent of voters respectively. During the 1990s Duke publicly distanced himself from his Klan past, but still put forward extreme views on racial issues. He continued to be a significant voice in Louisiana politics. In May 1999 he stood for the US House of Representatives in the state, securing 19 per cent of the vote. The same year he published his political autobiography, *My Awakening*. The book claimed that blacks were genetically inferior to whites, called for a separate homeland for blacks, and suggested that an Aryan revolution might be needed to secure the survival of the white race in the United States.

Although it was the best-known racist organization in the United States, the Ku Klux Klan suffered a major decline in both membership and political significance during the 1980s and the 1990s. The Klan was split by internal scandals and divisions. After Duke's 1979 resignation from the organization he was succeeded by Bill Wilkinson as the most widely recognized Klan spokesman. In 1984 Wilkinson lost his position as Imperial Wizard amid revelations that he had been an FBI informer. Following the demise of Wilkinson no one national Klan leader emerged. Instead, various small splinter groups all competed with each other to be recognized as the authentic Klan organization. All these groups suffered because of their outdated image. Klan robes and rituals seemed out of place at the end of the twentieth century.

Instead, right-wing extremists were attracted to a bewildering range of new anti-government or racist organizations, such as Tom Metzer's California-based White Aryan Resistance (WAR) and the Aryan Nations led by Richard Butler, with chapters in Florida, Arizona, Missouri, Michigan and Tennessee. In 1995 the American Jewish Committee estimated that there were some 10,000 active militia members in 30 states across America. In February 1999 the Southern Poverty Law Center in Montgomery identified 500 white supremacist organizations in the United States and 254 race-hate sites on the internet. Disparate and small in scale, these groups often shared a common allegiance to the racist religious movement Christian Identity. Central to Christian Identity's beliefs were claims that all Jews were the 'spawn of Satan', and that African Americans were only 'mud people' and not really human at all. White Anglo-Saxons, the true 'chosen people', had a divine responsibility to bring down the federal government or 'Zionist Occupation Government' (ZOG), and establish an all-white 'Kingdom of God' in the United States.

Under the influence of such teachings, extremist white organizations in the 1990s frequently engaged in acts of terrorism and violent race crimes. The most serious of these outrages was the bombing of a federal government building in Oklahoma City on 19 April 1995 by Timothy McVeigh. McVeigh's actions were partly influenced by his reading of a white supremacist novel, *The Turner Diaries* (1978).

On 7 June 1998, in another shocking incident, James Byrd, a 49-year-old African American, was brutally murdered in Jasper county, Texas. This was dubbed the 'death dragging' case in the media; Byrd was chained to a pick-up truck that was then driven at speed for nearly three miles. In February 1999, John William King, the first of three white supremacists to be put on trial for the murder, was convicted and sentenced to death. King had links with a racist group, the Confederate Knights of America.

On 2–4 July 1999 Benjamin Smith killed two people and injured nine others in Chicago in a series of racist shootings. Smith was associated with another white supremacist organization, the Illinois-based World Church of the Creator. Two supporters of the Church, Benjamin and James Matthews, were later linked to the killing of a homosexual couple in Sacramento, California on 1 July 1999. The large number of loosely connected extremist groups operating in the

United States made it harder for law-enforcement agencies to combat hate crimes in the 1990s. Lacking any effective national organization, racist groups offered up a 'leaderless resistance', with crimes usually carried out by lone individuals or isolated terrorist cells. The successful prosecution of any one cell or person thus had no impact on the wider problem of politically motivated racial or anti-government crime.

Changes in race relations were reflected in American popular culture during the last 25 years of the twentieth century. Between 1976 and 1980 the new trend of Disco dominated dance and music across the United States. Although popular among both whites and blacks, Disco had its origins in gay African American night-club culture. The superficial and gaudy sophistication of Disco night-clubs offered a temporary release from ghetto deprivation and national economic recession. This escapist appeal was memorably highlighted in the hit Hollywood film *Saturday Night Fever* (1977), starring John Travolta.

During the 1980s the growing marginalization and alienation of ghetto residents was witnessed in the rise of Hip-Hop. A black ghetto youth culture that originated in the late 1970s, Hip-Hop took a variety of cultural forms, most notably graffiti art, break-dancing and Rap music. In 1984 the album *Run DMC* by Run DMC became the first Rap record to achieve crossover success in the national music charts. Between 1987 and 1990 Public Enemy became the first superstar Rap group. In sharp contrast to Disco, Rap song lyrics dealt with the stark realities of everyday ghetto life. Rap music videos were typically shot in authentic inner-city locations.

Significantly, Rap started as an East-Coast phenomenon located primarily in New York City. In the 1990s the geographical centre of Rap shifted to California. This was seen in the rise of West-Coast Rappers Dr Dre, Snoop Doggy Dog, Niggaz Wit Attitude (NWA), Ice Cube and Tupac Shakur. The violent culture of Los Angeles and Watts ghetto gangs like the Crips and the Bloods became absorbed into Rap music. This was a factor in the emergence of Gangsta Rap, which promoted images of guns and violence as a means of artistic self-expression, as in Ice Cube's first solo album, *Amerikkka's Most Wanted* (1990). Gangsta tracks often engaged in revenge fantasies, with lyrics portraying black-on-white violence and simulated sounds of police officers being shot by black gunmen. Evocative and disturbing images of violence against women were even more common. Echoing the male chauvinism present within the earlier Black Power movement, this characteristic was an indication of the often aggressive sexism of Rap artists, most of whom were male.

Blurring the line between image and reality, some West-Coast Rap artists had violent personal backgrounds. Tupac Shakur had several criminal convictions, was shot and wounded in 1994, and, in September 1996, died of gunshot wounds sustained in another shooting incident. Dr Dre publicly assaulted the female Rapper and talk-show host Dee Barnes, and he appeared frequently in court. Snoop Doggy Dog was tried for and acquitted of murder.

The violent lifestyles of the ghetto were portrayed in a series of Hollywood films in the early 1990s, including John Singleton's *Boyz 'n the Hood* (1991), Melvin Van Peebles's *New Jack City* (1991), Allen and Albert Hughes's *Menace II Society* (1993) and *Clockers* (1995), directed by Spike Lee. Black filmmakers examined racial issues in a number of productions. *Panther* (1995), directed by Melvin Van Peebles, focused on the formation of the Black Panther Party for Self-Defense in the 1960s. *Do the Right Thing* (1989) by Spike Lee looked at the build-up of events leading to a race riot in New York City. Lee's *Jungle Fever* (1991) examined ghetto drug culture and an interracial sexual relationship. In 1992 Lee released his most ambitious work, *Malcolm X*, and in 1996 his more modest production *Get on the Bus* covered the experiences of participants in the Million Man March.

Mainstream Hollywood filmmakers were more wary of dealing with US race relations. In contrast to a number of films about the Vietnam War, there were few productions about the civil rights movement. One exception was *Mississippi Burning* (1988), by the British director Alan Parker, which was based on the 1964 murders of civil rights workers James Chaney, Andrew Goodman and Michael Schwerner in Mississippi. However, the film was attacked for its heroic depiction of the FBI and its lack of any central black characters.

Similar criticisms were made of films about the black freedom struggle in South Africa, *Cry Freedom* (1987), *A World Apart* (1988) and *A Dry White Season* (1989). Although they strongly denounced the apartheid regime in South Africa, these works focused more on the tribulations of white liberal campaigners against the system than the experiences of black South Africans. Two other films set in the region, *Out of Africa* (1985) and *Gorillas in the Mist* (1988), showed changing attitudes to gender, if not race. In these productions the Dark Continent was tamed by two lone white women rather than Tarzan, though still with the aid of faithful black camp followers.

Opportunities for black women in Hollywood continued to be few and far between in the 1980s and 1990s. Although there were some on-screen successes by musical celebrities, such as Grace Jones and Whitney Houston, Whoopi Goldberg was the only black actress to appear consistently in starring roles.

In contrast, there were an unprecedented number of black male superstars, including Denzel Washington, Morgan Freeman, Danny Glover, Wesley Snipes, Richard Pryor and Eddie Murphy. Nonetheless, racial taboos and stereotyping still persisted. The portrayal of explicit interracial sexual relations remained a largely no-go area in mainstream Hollywood film. This was despite more permissive attitudes towards on-screen sexuality as reflected in *Fatal Attraction* (1987), starring Michael Douglas and Glenn Close, and *Basic Instinct* (1992), with Michael Douglas and Sharon Stone.

Particularly common were 'buddy-buddy' movies, in which a black actor shared a leading role with a white co-star. Films in this category included *Trading Places* (1983) with Dan Ackroyd and Eddie Murphy, *Lethal Weapon* (1987) with Danny Glover and Mel Gibson, *Robin Hood, Prince of Thieves* (1991) with Kevin Costner and Morgan Freeman, *The Shawshank Redemption* (1994) with Tim Robbins and Morgan Freeman, and *Seven* (1995) with Brad Pitt and Morgan Freeman. In these productions the principal white characters were usually shown to have, or have been in, sexual relationships, and their social and family background was made clear. In contrast, their black co-stars were de-contextualized from African American culture and with little obvious sexual history, thereby avoiding any controversial examination of racial issues.

Some films made for television in the 1980s and 1990s did focus on racial issues and recent civil rights history. *Separate But Equal* (1991), with Sidney Poitier and Burt Lancaster, centred on the 1954 *Brown* v. *Topeka Board of Education* school desegregation decision. *Freedom Road: The Vernon Johns Story* (1994), with James Earl Jones, portrayed the life of Martin Luther King's radical predecessor as minister of the Dexter Avenue Baptist Church in Montgomery. One-off productions with low budgets and without the pressure for box-office success could more easily afford to look at controversial issues. This could even be a source of commercial appeal. Since they were unable to compete with lavish and complex Hollywood special effects, a choice of provocative subject matter, such as domestic violence, shocking legal cases, or racism, was an obvious alternative way for television filmmakers to attract audiences and hence sponsors.

In January 1977 the historical drama *Roots*, and the February 1979 sequel *Roots: The Next Generation*, followed the lives of black slaves and their descendants. A milestone in television history, the two mini-series attracted American viewing audiences of 140 million and 110 million respectively. Regarded at the time as daring and innovative, in hindsight *Roots* was less radical than it first appeared. The two series focused on the emotive struggle of one black family rather than engaging in a sustained criticism of American society. Despite their many trials and tribulations the family members still retained a belief in the American dream of ultimate equal opportunity for all in the pursuit of personal and material advancement.

The highly successful NBC comedy *The Cosby Show*, 1984–92, focused on a modern-day black family, the Huxtables, who had fulfilled the American dream. The fictional husband and wife, played by Bill Cosby and Phylicia Rashad, pursued rewarding careers as a physician and lawyer respectively. They enjoyed an affluent upper-middle-class lifestyle and had a loving stable relationship, both with each other and their intelligent, socially well-adjusted children. Proud of their racial heritage, the family seemed to be perfect role models for black Americans. Despite this, the show was sharply criticized by academic commentators. The Huxtables' material success suggested that by simple determination and hard work all black Americans could achieve such fulfilment. Family members rarely encountered direct racial prejudice or bigotry, and the problem of institutionalized racism in society was largely ignored. The affluent, idealized images of the Huxtables jarred uncomfortably with the real-life poverty and deprivation experienced by many African Americans. In a fitting irony, the broadcast of the last episode of *The Cosby Show*, in April 1992, coincided with the first night of the Rodney King riots in Los Angeles.

During the 1990s the most enduring images of race on network television were provided not by the imaginary utopia of *The Cosby*

*Show*, but by non-fictional news and documentary reports of racial discord. The 1991 US Senate hearings of Clarence Thomas, the 1992 Los Angeles riots, and the 1995 O. J. Simpson trial all received extensive television coverage, and provided poignant evidence of America's unresolved racial problems.

# Back to the future

There is a popular view that history repeats itself. The civil rights protests of the 1950s and 1960s, some 100 years after the Civil War, have been dubbed the 'Second Reconstruction'. To continue this analogy, the 1980s and the 1990s could be described as a second age of conservatism and accommodation, a period in which earlier gains, and the promise of a more enlightened age in US race relations, were lost or compromised in a return to more reactionary values.

Affirmative action programmes, once accepted as a long overdue remedy for racial injustice, were eroded by the courts, just as the Supreme Court had curtailed black civil and political rights in the 1890s. At the end of the nineteenth century, nativist organizations portrayed immigrant culture as harmful to US society, and scientific racism sought to prove the genetic inferiority of African Americans. In the late twentieth century, educational psychologist Arthur Jensen and New York City College professor Michael Levin asserted that blacks were intellectually inferior to whites. Dr Leonard Jeffries, an African American professor at New York City College, claimed that blacks were victims of a Jewish and Mafia conspiracy. If the Ku Klux Klan appeared dated and unfashionable in the 1980s and the 1990s, its racist views were taken up by a range of new white supremacist organizations.

During the last years of the twentieth century, many of the leading figures of the civil rights movement and the Black Power years passed away into history. In 1989 Black Panther founder Huey Newton was killed in a street shooting in Oakland. In May 1998 Newton's co-leader of the Panthers, Eldridge Cleaver, died in Los Angeles after a prolonged struggle against drug addiction. Betty Shabbaz died after a house fire in June 1997, and in November 1998 Black Power icon Stokely Carmichael (Kwane Ture) died of prostate cancer in Guinea, West Africa. In July 1999 James Farmer, co-founder and former head of CORE, died aged 79 after several years of ill health. He had been the last survivor of the 'Big Four' civil rights leaders of the 1960s, following the death of SCLC president Martin Luther King in 1968, Urban League National Director Whitney Young in 1971, and NAACP Executive Secretary Roy Wilkins in 1981. A symbolic final link with the civil rights movement was broken with Farmer's passing.

Over time new leaders, Jesse Jackson, Kweisi Mfume and Louis Farrakhan, emerged to take the places of the departed legends. Like their illustrious predecessors they struggled to overcome the many and depressing problems that continued to be faced by African Americans. This was inevitable. All leaders, however great their individual talents, are the products of the age into which they are born. They are more shaped by society than they are able to shape it.

In 1895, the Atlanta Compromise speech established Booker T. Washington as the best-known and most influential race leader of his day. In a period of worsening race relations, Washington advocated a conservative programme of industrial education and economic self-help. A century later the Million Man March of 1995 confirmed Louis Farrakhan's national status as an African American spokesperson. In another era of racial conservatism, Farrakhan's ideas echoed those put forward by Washington. Albeit in black nationalist rhetoric, Farrakhan called on African Americans to recognize the need for thrift, a stronger work ethic, and a return to family values. During his lifetime Booker T. Washington was attacked by northern black critics as conservative and backward-looking. In 1999 Louis Farrakhan celebrated his sixty-sixth birthday following several years of health problems. Like Washington before him, he appeared more a figure of the century just gone than a visionary leader for the new one to come.

The year 1999 saw another significant birthday as the NAACP commemorated the ninetieth year of its existence. Its founding vision of an integrated society with racial equality seemed, in many respects, to be as remote as ever. By the end of the twentieth century, the study of African American history had achieved mainstream recognition and respect as an academic subject. At the same time historical problems faced by black Americans remained unresolved. African Americans continued to suffer economic and social deprivation. Despite the important gains made since the 1960s they were still under-represented in terms of political office holding at all levels of society.

In the 1990s two-thirds of all black students attended predominantly minority schools. Legal, or *de jure*, segregation may have passed away, but *de facto* economic and residential segregation remained. Washington, DC, the nation's capital, in common with other leading urban centres in the United States, continued to be a city divided along racial lines. The portrayal of blacks in popular culture continued to be stereotyped and unrealistic.

In 1960, during the first of his televised presidential election debates with Richard Nixon, John F. Kennedy compared the prospects of black and white children. He observed that a black baby had 'half as much chance to go through high school . . . one-third as much chance to get through college . . . a third as much chance to be a professional . . . about half as much chance to own a house' and 'about four times as much chance' of being out of work.

During the 1990s over one-half of all of black children continued to live in poverty. A black baby was over twice as likely as a white baby to die before its first birthday. More black men in their twenties were in prison, on parole or on probation than attended college. The average black family earned only 56–60 per cent of the income enjoyed by their white counterparts. A black man was six times more likely to be murdered than a white man. In the words of John F. Kennedy, America 'can do better'.

# Supreme Court cases cited in the text

*Plessy* v. *Ferguson* (1896)
*Williams* v. *Mississippi* (1898)
*Buchanan* v. *Warley* (1917)
*Missouri ex rel. Gaines* v. *Canada* (1938)
*Smith* v. *Allwright* (1944)
*Sweatt* v. *Painter* (1950)
*Brown* v. *the Topeka Board of Education* (1954)
*Boynton* v. *Virginia* (1960)
*Alexander* v. *Holmes County* (1969)
*Giggs* v. *Duke Power Company* (1971)
*Swann* v. *Charlotte-Mecklenberg Board of Education* (1971)
*Millican* v. *Bradley* (1974)
*Regents of the University of California* v. *Bakke* (1978)
*Fullilove* v. *Klutznick* (1980)
*Bob Jones University* v. *US* (1983)
*Adarond Construction* v. *Pera* (1995)

# Select bibliography

## Books

Bogle, D. *Toms, Coons, Mulattoes, Mammies and Bucks: An Interpretative History of Blacks in American Films*, New York: Continuum, 1990.

Boyd, T. *Am I Black Enough for You? Popular Culture from the 'Hood' and Beyond*, Bloomington: Indiana University Press, 1997.

Branch, T. *Parting the Waters: Martin Luther King and the Civil Rights Movement, 1954–63*, London: Macmillan, 1991.

Branch, T. *Pillar of Fire: America in the King Years, 1963–65*, New York: Simon and Schuster, 1998.

Brauer, C. M. *John F. Kennedy and the Second Reconstruction*, New York: Columbia University Press, 1977.

Brown, E. *A Taste of Power: A Black Woman's Story*, New York: Anchor, 1994.

Burk, R. F. *The Eisenhower Administration and Black Civil Rights*, Knoxville: University of Tennessee Press, 1984.

Burner, E. R. *and gently he shall lead them: Robert Parrish Moses and Civil Rights in Mississippi*, New York: New York University Press, 1994.

Bushart, H. L., J. R. Craig and M. Barnes, *Soldiers of God: White Supremacists and their Holy War for America*, New York: Kensington Books, 1998.

Carmichael, S. and C. V. Hamilton, *Black Power: The Politics of Liberation in America*, London: Jonathan Cape, 1967.

Carson, C. *In Struggle: SNCC and the Black Awakening of the 1960s*, Cambridge, MA: Harvard University Press, 1981.

Carson, C. (ed.) *The Eyes on the Prize Civil Rights Reader, 1954–1990*, London: Penguin, 1991.

Carson, C. *The Autobiography of Martin Luther King*, Boston: Little Brown and Co., 1999.

Clarke, J. H. (ed.) *Malcolm X: The Man and his Times*, New York: African World Press, 1990.

Cleaver, E. *Soul on Ice*, New York: Dell Publishing, 1992.

Cone, J. H. *Martin and Malcolm and America: A Dream or a Nightmare*, New York: Orbis Books, 1996.

Cook, R. *Sweet Land of Liberty? The African-American Struggle for Civil Rights in the Twentieth Century*, London: Longman, 1998.

Crawford, V. L., J. A. Rouse and B. Woods (eds) *Women in the Civil Rights Movement: Trailblazers and Torchbearers, 1941–1965*, Bloomington: Indiana University Press, 1993.

Cronon, E. D. *Black Moses: The Story of Marcus Garvey and the Universal Negro Improvement Association*, London: University of Wisconsin Press, 1969.

Cruse, H. *The Crisis of the Negro Intellectual*, New York: William Morrow, 1984.

DeCaro, L. A. *On the Side of my People: A Religious Life of Malcolm X*, New York: New York University Press, 1996.

Dyson, M. E. *Making Malcolm: The Myth and Meaning of Malcolm X*, Oxford: Oxford University Press, 1995.

Ellison, M. *The Black Experience: American Blacks since 1865*, London: B. T. Batsford, 1974.

Ely, M. P. *The Adventures of Amos 'n' Andy: A Social History of an American Phenomenon*, New York: The Free Press, 1991.

Fairclough, A. *To Redeem the Soul of America: The Southern Christian Leadership Conference and Martin Luther King, Jr.*, Athens: University of Georgia Press, 1987.

Fairclough, A. *Race and Democracy in the Civil Rights Struggle in Louisiana, 1915–1972*, Athens: University of Georgia Press, 1995.

Foner, E. *Reconstruction: America's Unfinished Revolution, 1863–77*, New York: Harper and Row, 1988.

Franklin, J. H. and A. Meier (eds) *Black Leaders of the Twentieth Century*, Urbana: University of Illinois Press, 1982.

Franklin, J. H. and A. A. Moss, *From Slavery to Freedom: A History of African Americans*, New York: McGraw-Hill, 1994.

Garrow, D. J. *Bearing the Cross: Martin Luther King, Jr., and the Southern Christian Leadership Conference*, New York: Vintage Books, 1988.

Gavins, R. *The Perils and Prospects of Southern Black Leadership: Gordon Blaine Hancock, 1884–1970*, Durham: Duke University Press, 1993.

Haley, A. *The Autobiography of Malcolm X*, London: Penguin Books, 1968.

Harlan, L. R. *Booker T. Washington: The Making of a Black Leader, 1856–1901*, Oxford: Oxford University Press, 1972.

Harlan, L. R. *Booker T. Washington: The Wizard of Tuskegee, 1901–1915*, Oxford: Oxford University Press, 1983.

Hill, D. M. and P. S. Herrnson (eds) *The Clinton Presidency: The First Term, 1992–1996*, London: Macmillan Press, 1999.

Horne, G. *Fire This Time: The Watts Uprising and the 1960s*, Charlottesville: University Press of Virginia, 1995.

James, W. *Holding Aloft the Banner of Ethiopia: Caribbean Radicalism in Early Twentieth Century America*, London: Verso Books, 1998.

Jhally, S. and J. Lewis, *Enlightened Racism: The Cosby Show, Audiences, and the Myth of the American Dream*, Boulder: Westview Press, 1992.

Leab, D. J. *From Sambo to Superspade: The Black Experience in Motion Pictures*, London: Secker and Warburg, 1973.

Lemann, N. *The Promised Land: The Great Migration and How it Changed America*, London: Macmillan, 1991.

Lewis, D. L. *W. E. B. DuBois: Biography of a Race, 1868–1919*, New York: Henry Holt, 1993.

Lewis, D. L. *W. E. B. DuBois: A Reader*, New York: Henry Holt, 1995.

Litwack, L. and A. Meier (eds) *Black Leaders of the Nineteenth Century*, Urbana: University of Illinois Press, 1988.

MacDonald, J. F. *Blacks and White TV: Afro-Americans in Television since 1948*, Chicago: Nelson Hall, 1983.

McFeely, W. S. *Frederick Douglass*, New York: W. W. Norton, 1991.

McKnight, G. B. *The Last Crusade: Martin Luther King, Jr., the FBI, and the Poor People's Campaign*, Oxford: Westview Press, 1998.

McNeil, G. R. *Groundwork: Charles Hamilton Houston and the*

*Struggle for Civil Rights*, Philadelphia: University of Pennsylvania Press, 1983.

Marable, M. *Race, Reform and Rebellion: The Second Reconstruction in Black America, 1945–1990*, London: Macmillan Education, 1991.

Marable, M. *Beyond Black and White: Transforming African-American Politics*, London: Verso, 1995.

Marable, M. *Black Liberation in Conservative America*, Boston: South End Press, 1997.

Marable, M. *Black Leadership*, New York: Columbia University Press, 1998.

Marks, C. *Farewell – We're Good and Gone: The Great Black Migration*, Bloomington: Indiana University Press, 1989.

Martin, T. *Race First: The Ideological and Organizational Struggles of Marcus Garvey and the UNIA*, Westport: Greenwood Press, 1976.

Martin Riches, W. T. *The Civil Rights Movement: Struggle and Resistance*, London: Macmillan, 1997.

Meier, A. and E. Rudwick, *CORE: A Study in the Civil Rights Movement, 1942–68*, Urbana: University of Illinois Press, 1975.

Morris, A. *The Origins of the Civil Rights Movement: Black Communities Organizing for Change*, London: Collier Macmillan, 1984.

O'Reilly, K. *Nixon's Piano: Presidents and Racial Politics from Washington to Clinton*, New York: The Free Press, 1995.

Perry, B. *Malcolm, the Life of a Man Who Changed America*, New York: Station Hill, 1991.

Pfeffer, P. A. *Philip Randolph: Pioneer of the Civil Rights Movement*, Baton Rouge: Louisiana State University Press, 1990.

Ralph, J. R. *Northern Protest: Martin Luther King, Jr., Chicago and the Civil Rights Movement*, Cambridge, MA: Harvard University Press, 1993.

Reed, A. L. *The Jesse Jackson Phenomenon: The Crisis of Purpose in Afro-American Politics*, New Haven: Yale University Press, 1986.

Ridgeway, J. *Blood in the Face: The Ku Klux Klan, Aryan Nations, Nazi Skinheads and the Rise of a New White Culture*, New York: Thunders Mouth, 1995.

Rose, T. *Black Noise: Rap Music and Black Culture in Contemporary America*, Hanover, New Hampshire: Wesleyan University Press, 1994.

Sarat, A. (ed.) *Race, Law and Culture: Reflections on Brown v Board of Education*, Oxford: Oxford University Press, 1997.

Seale, B. *Seize the Time: The Story of the Black Panther Party and Huey Newton*, Baltimore: Black Classics, 1991.

Sernett, M. *Bound for the Promised Land: African American Religion and the Great Migration*, Durham: Duke University Press, 1997.

Singh, R. *The Farrakhan Phenomenon: Race, Reaction and the Paranoid Style in American Politics*, Washington, DC: Georgetown University Press, 1997.

Sharpton, A. and A. Walton, *Go and Tell Pharaoh: The Autobiography of the Reverend Al Sharpton*, New York: Doubleday, 1996.

Sitkoff, H. *A New Deal for Blacks: The Emergence of Civil Rights as a National Issue*, New York: Oxford University Press, 1978.

Smock, R. W. (ed.) *Booker T. Washington in Perspective: Essays of Louis R. Harlan*, London: University Press of Mississippi, 1988.

Southern, D. W. *Gunnar Myrdal and Black–White Relations: The Use and Abuse of an American Dilemma, 1944–1969*, Baton Rouge: Louisiana State University Press, 1987.

Southern, E. *The Music of Black Americans: A History*, 3rd edn, New York: W. W. Norton, 1997.

Stein, J. *The World of Marcus Garvey: Race and Class in Modern Society*, Baton Rouge: Louisiana State University Press, 1986.

Sullivan, P. *Days of Hope: Race and Democracy in the New Deal Era*, Chapel Hill: University of North Carolina Press, 1996.

Torres, S. *Living Color: Race and Television in the United States*, Durham: Duke University Press, 1998.

Trotter, J. W. (ed.) *The Great Migration in Historical Perspective*, Bloomington: Indiana University Press, 1991.

Van Deburg, W. L. *New Day in Babylon: The Black Power Movement and American Culture, 1965–75*, Chicago: University of Chicago Press, 1992.

Van Woodward, C. *The Strange Career of Jim Crow*, 3rd revised edn, Oxford: Oxford University Press, 1974.

Vincent, T. G. *Black Power and the Garvey Movement*, Berkeley: The Ramparts Press, 1971.

Wade, W. C. *The Fiery Cross: The Ku Klux Klan in America*, New York: Simon and Schuster, 1987.

Ward, B. *Just My Soul Responding: Rhythm and Blues, Black Consciousness and Race Relations*, London: UCL Press, 1998.

Watts, J. *God, Harlem, USA: The Father Divine Story*, Berkeley: University of California Press, 1992.

Weiss, N. J. *Farewell to the Party of Lincoln: Black Politics in the Age of FDR*, Princeton: Princeton University Press, 1983.

White, J. *Black Leadership in America from Booker T. Washington to Jesse Jackson*, 2nd edn, Harlow: Longman, 1990.

Williamson, J. *The Crucible of Race: Black–White Relations in the American South Since Emancipation*, Oxford: Oxford University Press, 1984.

Wilson, W. J. *The Declining Significance of Race*, London: University of Chicago Press, 1978.

Wolfenstein, E. *The Victims of Democracy: Malcolm X and the Black Revolution*, London: Free Association Books, 1989.

Wynn, N. A. *The Afro-American and the Second World War*, London: Holmes and Meier, 1993.

## Television and Video Documentaries

Blackside, Inc. *Eyes on the Prize*, 1990.

Riggs, M. T., director and V. Kleiman, producer, *Color Adjustment*, 1991.

## Internet websites

*CNN.*

*The Congress of Racial Equality (CORE).*

*NAACP Online.*

*The New York Times.*

*The National Urban League (NUL).*

# Index